D0605141

WOMAN ALIVE

What Makes Men Tick

by Portia Beers

 Aldus Books London

Series Coordinator: John Mason
Design Director: Guenther Radtke
Picture Editor: Peter Cook
Editors: Ann Craig
         Mary Senechal
Copy Editor: Mitzi Bales
Research: Elizabeth Lake
          Lynette Trotter
          Sarah Waters
Consultants: Beppie Harrison
             Jo Sandilands

Contents

Men! Tough-minded and tender-hearted, foolish and wise, stubborn and impulsive, thoughtless and considerate—they can be maddening and they can be marvelous. They can also be very mystifying, for, as most of us have discovered, there is something about the way a man's mind works that is altogether different from a woman's. This, however, has never prevented men from writing books about women. So here's a book—by a woman—about men. Light-hearted and serious by turns, it makes no claims to being the last word on the subject. But it does provide some fascinating food for thought. You yourself may agree or disagree with it, but one thing is certain: when the man in your life sees you reading a book called **What Makes Men Tick,** *he's bound to be more than a little interested in just what it has to say!*

The Male Animal

How would you define manhood? For a start, you'd probably list all the qualities traditionally associated with male dominance: strength, virility, tough-mindedness, authority, aggressiveness, and fearlessness.

Below: the original caveman—hunter, provider, protector—the archetypical he-man.

Right: in the Middle Ages, women were regarded as chattel, and husbands believed that they had every right to beat their wives.

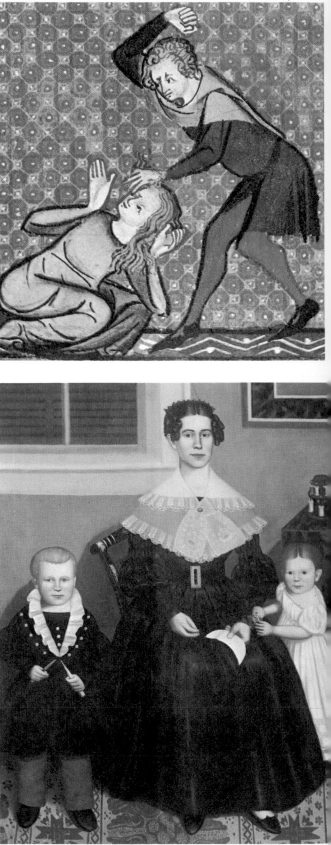

Left: an early American frontiersman, trekking across country, with his Indian wife dutifully following a few paces behind him.

Below left: detail from an early American painting of a typical family group around 1839. The term "head of the family" was taken very seriously during the stern and moralistic years of the 19th century, and fathers were held in awe by their children.

Below: Steve McQueen is the screen's embodiment of total masculinity. Tough and reckless, he seems to symbolize virility.

Behind Every Man...

From a very long time back, people have recognized the importance of women's influence over men. Behind the scenes, many a woman has wielded power through a man.

Above: Adam and Eve leaving the Garden of Eden—and we know who gets blamed.

Above right: Catherine de Médicis, the wife of one French king and mother of three more. She ruled them—and the country.

Below left: Lady Macbeth, literature's most notorious female plotter, urging her weak husband to kill the king and take his place.

Above: Eleanor and Franklin D. Roosevelt. Though he was president, she was the driving force behind many of his decisions.

Left: Jennie Churchill, the strong-willed mother of Winston Churchill (on her left).

Below: Nicholas II of Russia, with his wife Alexandra. Her misguided loyalties, coupled with his weakness, brought their downfall.

Men as Lovers

Love is supposed to be a woman's province, but some of the world's most famous and flamboyant lovers have been men. In fact, many a well-known man's chief claim to fame rests on his romantic or sexual exploits.

Right: Louis XIV of France, known as "the Sun King." The long list of his mistresses suggests that he also shone in the boudoir.

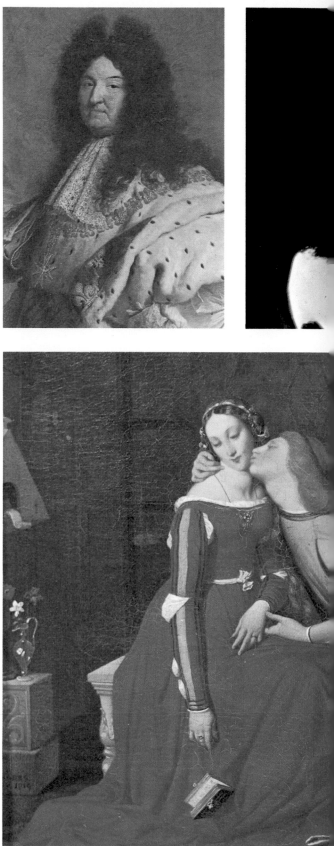

Above: Casanova, perhaps the best-known lover of them all. His hundreds of amorous conquests are recounted in loving detail in his twelve-volume autobiography.

Below left: Paolo and Francesca, a pair of young lovers whose tragic story was immortalized by Dante. Francesca was the wife of Paolo's brother, seen here about to kill him.

Left: Rudolph Valentino, that movie idol of the silent screen whose flashing eyes, extravagant gestures, and ardent love scenes caused many a feminine heart to beat faster.

Below: Mick Jagger, male sex symbol of our age. In many ways, his effect on female fans is similar to that of Valentino's; his aggressive sexuality has a totally direct appeal.

Men Without Women

Every age has had its own organizations for men only. Their purpose has varied widely, but in every case, the exclusion of women seems to have given them a special appeal.

Below: a Crusader. The comradeship of fighting men is central to the male mystique.

Right: Franciscan friars of the 15th century. Commitment to a life of celibacy can be the ultimate test of a man's self-discipline.

Below: a group of 19th-century Freemasons. Membership in this exclusive male organization has brought satisfaction to many men.

Above right: a parade of Shriners, wearing their traditional red fezzes. Their all-male association is an offshoot of Freemasonry.

Right: a member of the Gay Liberation Front. Male homosexuality is not new, of course, but this demand for recognition is.

Below: what could be more thoroughly male than football? Here, beefy football players represent the epitome of modern masculinity.

In a Man's World

"Never underestimate the power of a woman". Though traditionally a woman's place has been in the home, there have always been women who have managed to succeed in fields chiefly reserved for men.

Below: Joan of Arc, who led the French army to free her people from English rule.

Right: Elizabeth I, Queen of England. Shrewd and tough-minded, she ruled better than many of her male predecessors.

Right: Marie and Pierre Curie. Her contribution to the study of radium won her a Nobel prize after the death of her husband.

Below: Indira Ghandi, stateswoman *par excellence,* here conferring with leaders Kosygin of the Soviet and Tito of Yugoslavia.

Above and below: can women play an equal part in the aerospace program? Susan Oliver (above), who flew a record-breaking transatlantic flight in 1967, and Mary Wallace Funk (below), who has passed all the grueling tests required of an astronaut, would answer with an emphatic "yes".

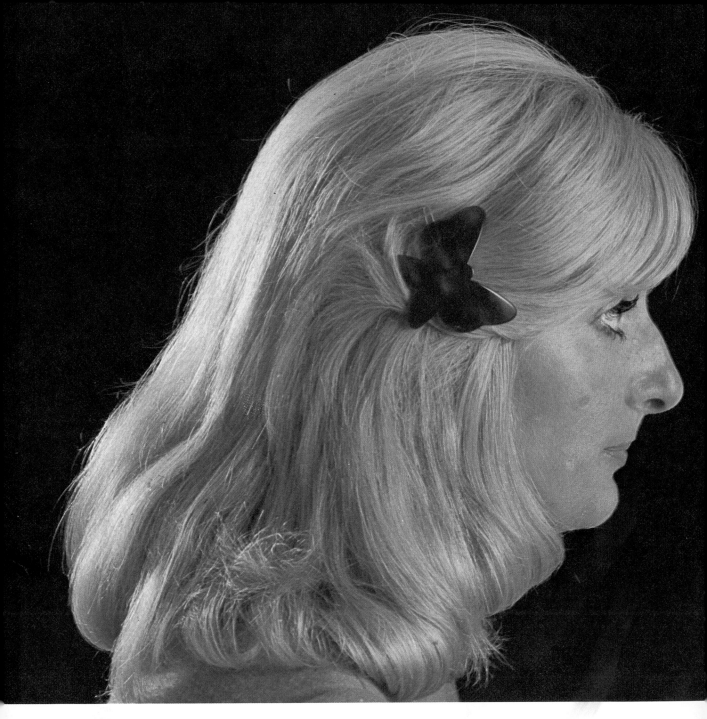

Them and Us
1

All men are to some extent mysterious to every woman. Male pursuits are mysterious to her, male ambitions are mysterious to her, male sexuality is mysterious to her. Even the man she loves and marries—her husband and the father of her children—even he will always remain in some ways as foreign to her as a Martian.

Not surprisingly, each of these statements could be reversed, for it is equally true that all women are to some extent mysterious

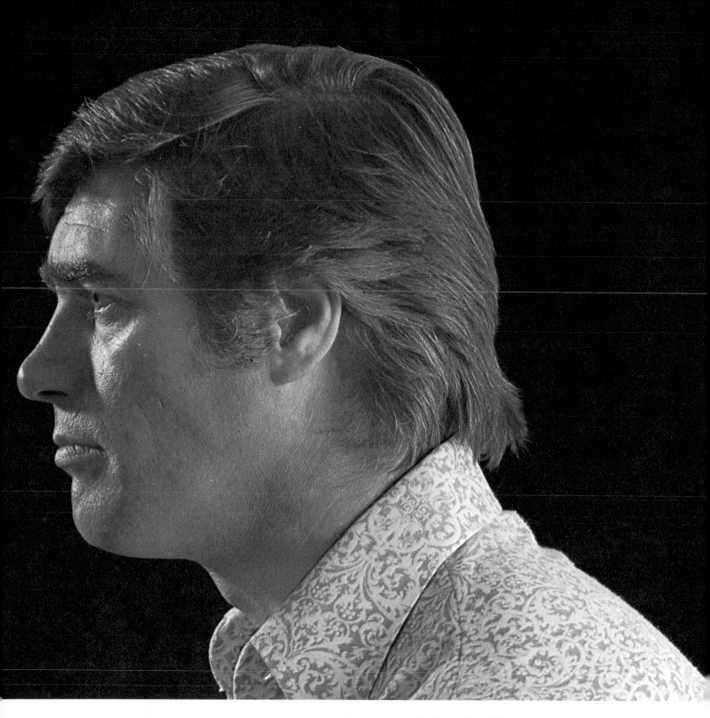

to every man. In the ultimate sense, it could also be said that no individual is completely knowable by another, simply because each of us possesses a mind and heart unique to ourselves. But apart from the personality differences that make each of us unique, there's another, more basic difference that divides all of humanity right down the middle: namely, the difference between men and women.

To begin with, male and female bodies

He's annoyed. She's bewildered. It's yet another skirmish in the "battle of the sexes". Men and women need each other and belong together, but the mystery that attracts can also divide them.

are constructed differently. That much is obvious. So is the reason why: that we may beget children and thus ensure the survival of the race. It is also obvious that, because man and woman are made differently, neither can fully understand the powers,

The family has always been the central unit of society, weathering all the storms of history from the Stone Age to the Space Age. Despite its modern critics, it shows every sign of surviving—even thriving on—the new pressures it faces today. What gives the family this extraordinary resilience? Simply its unique capacity to meet and adapt to our basic human needs.

Above: a Brazilian family of primitive Indians.

Left: a modern American family—outwardly different from their Brazilian counterparts, but playing the same fundamental family roles.

pleasures, and weaknesses of the other's body. They may feel the power, give the pleasure, learn the weakness of the other, but neither man nor woman can ever know precisely what it is like to *be* the other, at least in physical terms.

All this really goes without saying. It is simply one of life's "givens," and we don't question it. What we are beginning to question these days is, what makes men and women so different psychologically? That men's bodies, voices, and ways of moving are different from ours, we take for granted. That they experience sex differently from us, we also take for granted. But why is it that they think and feel, hope and dream differently? Why do they respond to people and problems differently? Why should there be characteristically different masculine and feminine views on life in general and love in particular? Are these dissimilarities in mind and heart simply a matter of social conditioning, or are they instinctive and inborn?

Traditionally, in primitive and sophisticated societies alike, the differences between men and women were accepted as an intrinsic part of living, a kind of basic blueprint, in fact, for the way life should be led. The simple fact of being born a male or a female more or less determined an individual's roles, rights, and responsibilities. In practical terms, the differences between the sexes served as a handy guideline for the division of labor, and as a ready-made pattern for the care and teaching of children.

In the past, this clear-cut division of roles according to sex seemed so natural, and usually worked so well (despite the usual misunderstandings and complaints on both sides), that no one bothered to examine it very carefully. It was just accepted as part and parcel of The Way Things Are.

Increasingly, however, in our own hectic and rapidly changing society, this traditional acceptance is breaking down. Many people, both men and women, are beginning to question the idea that the mere accident of gender should play so absolute a part in determining our personalities, roles, and expectations. Many women in particular these days are critical of what they call an outdated and essentially unfair division of life's possibilities. Some of them complain that the bearing and rearing of children is not sufficiently fulfilling. Others say that they are tired of being expected to keep the home fires burning while their husbands meet the challenges—and the temptations —of the larger world outside. Others decry the kind of "Playboy philosophy" that encourages men to regard women primarily as sex objects. Still others are up in arms against the kind of childhood training that teaches girls to consider themselves as somehow inferior to boys.

Many men are sympathetic to this indictment of sexual inequality, but there are others who, with some justification, point out that being a man isn't all that enviable. After all, they say, who is it that's expected to bear all the major financial responsibilities? Who works and slaves to provide his family with the necessities and luxuries of life? Who is it that gets ulcers worrying about his job, not only because it's his living, but also because it's his life, the basic touchstone of his self-image? Who is it that's expected to take up arms in time of war, risking life and limb to prove his courage and fight for his country? On still another level (though men are rarely so outspoken about this one), who is it whose very sexuality is put to the ultimate test, and in a far more obvious way than a woman's, every time he has sex?

People have argued time and time again

20

"WOMEN OF THE WORLD UNITE!" The movement for women's rights has galvanized women all over the world to protest against sexual inequality in various areas of life. These pictures were taken at a massive Women's Lib demonstration on the streets of a major American city. Among the demonstrators were women of every age and point of view—including the opposition, whose defensive battle cry was: "MEN OUR MASTERS".

21

about which is the easier social and personal role to play. In recent years, too, an increasing number of men and women have tried their hand at switching the roles of provider and homemaker. In some cases, it's done out of necessity: the wife works to support the family and the husband looks after the kids, simply because he's been laid off from work and is having a hard time finding another job. In other cases, it's a matter of sheer convenience: husband and wife swap the functions of wage earner and housekeeper for no other reason than because it suits them.

Even so dramatic a reversal of roles, however, doesn't seem to affect the fundamental psychological differences between the husband and wife. He is a man, she is a woman, and the differences between them go far deeper than the question of who's earning the money and who's looking after the kids. It goes deeper, too, than the issue of "who wears the pants" in the family. It even goes deeper than—though it is rooted in—the physical symbols of their sexuality. Perplexingly, the difference between men and women lies, at its deepest level, in the way they think and feel— about themselves, about those they love, about the work they do, and about what they can expect from life. The question is, do these fundamental differences spring solely from the fact that they were created male and female? Are the differences between the masculine and feminine approach to life absolutely dependent on sexual identity?

"A man is ruled by his head, a woman by her heart." So goes the old saying. It's one of those generalizations we've heard so often that we accept it as gospel, just as we accept the old saw about women being intuitive, while men are logical. Putting aside for a moment the glaring lapses in logic men seem to be prone to (we all know how maddeningly impulsive and downright unreasonable they can be at times), just how intuitive are women?

More often than not, what men like to

Slowly but surely, our rigid concepts of male and female roles are beginning to change. Many women are learning to excel in fields once only open to men, and many men are discovering talents for child care that they never thought they had.

Above: this young woman has proved herself in the competitive world of civil engineering.

Right: the sight of a young father feeding his baby is becoming increasingly common as men play a greater part in raising their children.

Right: coffee clatches like this have become a tradition among American women. With their husbands at work and their children at school, they can sit down for a couple of hours, relax, and talk about the things that concern them most.

Below: women lunching together in 17th-century Holland. No doubt much of their conversation would seem familiar to the woman of today. Certainly, they, too, enjoyed the opportunity to get together and talk to their hearts' content while their menfolk were away.

call feminine intuition is simply native intelligence applied to areas that men are rarely called upon to consider. There is nothing particularly intuitive, for example, about baking bread, caring for a baby, knitting a sweater, holding a dinner party, or coping with a clutch of fractious children. These are areas in which women have been trained, and in which they have learned, through trial and error, to succeed. One might well ask whether, when women excel in other areas—such as finance, medicine, or the arts—they are demonstrating their intuition, or simply applying intelligence and education to the job at hand?

Women are probably no more instinctively intuitive than men. If women seem to possess in greater measure the ability to size up a situation fast, it's because they've always been encouraged to do so. In the same way as quick reflexes are encouraged in an athlete, women are expected, from the time they are little girls, to be athletes in the emotional field. They realize very early that their role in life—as daughter, girlfriend, employee, fiancée, wife, and mother—will require a keen awareness of other people's personalities and moods. Because their success as women will largely depend on their ability to cope with various human relationships, they develop a special skill at personal diplomacy, sensitivity, and flexibility. Men, too, might exercise these skills if their occupations required it; but in the main, a man's job chiefly requires him to deal with objects, facts and figures. Because this is the case, he is encouraged from boyhood onward to reason things out, to weigh and measure, consider and calculate, rather than intuit. This doesn't, of course, prevent him from occasionally playing a hunch, and what's a hunch but an intuition, pure and simple?

The division of labor established at the dawn of housekeeping still exists to a large extent and still serves to make men and women different in their interests and pastimes. Take gossiping, for example, an

25

activity that seems to have an exclusively feminine aura about it. In fact, what is called gossip is no more than women exchanging views and observations about various human relationships. It is, after all, an area in which they are not only trained, but expected to specialize. As domestic diplomats, amateur sociologists, and instant psychotherapists all rolled into one, is it any wonder that they tend to discuss the pleasures, puzzles, and problems of their specialty when they get together?

In the world of men, interpersonal relationships usually take second place to considerations involving machines and methods, facts and figures, tools and tactics. He may be a computer expert, a rancher, a car mechanic, a politician, a salesman, or an artist. Whatever he is, when he says he doesn't like to gossip, he is only saying that he prefers to discuss what's happening in his trade or profession, or the comparative merits of different teams and players, or the pressing problems of inflation, taxation, and house payments. For him, it's the most natural thing in the world to discuss work, sports, and finance; he feels uncomfortable, even somewhat out of his depth, discussing the personalities and relationships of people he knows. So, when the conversation gets around to what he calls gossip, he leaves his wife and her friends to it, while he and *his* friends talk about serious matters—such as what's wrong with the car, or wrong with the country. But as every woman knows, it's still gossip no matter what the men like to call it.

Alas, the gulf between masculine and feminine is rarely crossed via the simple bridge of friendship. Among the men in a woman's life—among these creatures whose bodies, passions, and powers are different; whose habits, interests, and pastimes are different; whose expectations, ambitions, and courage are different; whose very experience of everyday life is different— among these males, a woman can only very rarely find a friend as she understands the meaning of the word. Nor would she

26

Left: here's one place you're sure to find more men than women. When women want to talk, they either pick up the phone or meet in one another's homes. But a male get-together is usually outside the home in a club or bar.

Below: a group of 18th-century men living it up in a tavern. It's a far more riotous scene than the one above but, like their modern counterparts, the men are busy drinking. Liquor has been a staple ingredient of male gatherings since time immemorial.

really want to relate to the men she knows as she does to members of her own sex. She knows that one of the chief attractions between the sexes is the very mystery that makes simple friendship practically impossible.

Even when a woman enters the essentially masculine world of business and excels in it, the mystery surrounding the opposite sex remains. A successful career woman has been known to be awed by the uncanny wisdom of an electrician. She may consider her ability to be a mere fluke, but his is an intrinsic part of the great, mysterious masculine heritage that is forever closed to her. He cannot bear a child, but she cannot fix a faulty lamp, repair the toaster she uses every morning, or comprehend the workings of the iron she presses her husband's shirts with. She has never been called upon to understand these things; she doubts whether she really could, even if they were carefully explained to her. The ability to understand how things work, and to fix them when they go wrong —all this is part of the male mystique. It is also part of the "don't bother your pretty little head about it" attitude, which tends, unfortunately, to widen the gap between men and women. Perhaps, too, it is inevitable, because for a woman, any man doing a job—be it management, engineering, medicine, farming, truck driving, journalism, the law, or whatever—automatically assumes some of the mystery and power she associated with her father when she was a child.

Both men and women, who are usually very clear-sighted about members of their own sex, are frequently unable to see any failings in a member of the opposite sex. After all, where there are mysteries on one side, there are bound to be fantasies on the other. If you receive an unexpected package in the mail your imagination will fill it with something beautiful. Nine times out of ten, it turns out to be samples of a new soap powder, and the tenth time, a knitted tea cosy from your Aunt Mabel.

Why should a man be all thumbs in the kitchen? Why should a woman feel lost when her car breaks down? Neither cooking nor mechanics really has to be the exclusive pre- serve of one sex or the other. It has just been more convenient to see things that way. These two pictures illustrate the traditional view of male and female limita- tions outside their own spheres: he's cheated in buying the cake; and she can't seem to tell one end of the exhaust pipe from the other.

But even bitter experience won't stop your imagination from filling the next box with something special, something beautiful.

Because men and women look, love, and live differently, they cannot help filling in the gaps in their knowledge of one another with sheer fantasy. How often have you seen a woman fall in love with an out-and-out scoundrel—a liar, lady killer, or hard-drinking gambler, for example—and found that it was impossible to tell her so? Love isn't really blind. It's just astigmatic, and can blur even the most glaring faults until they become special virtues. In fact, it's tremendously difficult for any of us to see in a member of the opposite sex exactly what's there: another real and very vulnerable human being.

Relationships between the sexes are changing more rapidly than any nation's inflation spiral, but the well-publicized sexual freedom and personal honesty of the young belong to only a few. Most men and women still have to think hard about their relationships with the opposite sex, because those relationships, so cluttered with emotional hardware on both sides, usually require more steering than a simple friendship with a member of the same sex.

In the long run, of course, it's not so much the differences between the sexes that worry us—they're what make the world go round, after all—as the misunderstandings that arise from them. Very little, at least at present, can be done to change the fact that men and women often have conflicting views on life, love, and the pursuit of happiness. Nothing at all, thankfully, can change the fact that humanity *is* divided into men and women—delightfully, irritatingly, mystifyingly different from one another in so many ways. What can change, and is already beginning to change, is the depth of our understanding—not only of ourselves, but of the men we love.

As their roles change and the comfortable myths they grew up with melt away, men and women need each other's understanding as never before.

The Making of a Woman

2

Biologically speaking, the female and male of a pair of mixed twins cease to have a great deal in common months before they open their eyes to daylight for the first time. And, as Nature gives them the inner chemistry and outer anatomy that marks their male and female sexuality while they are still in the womb, so custom, tradition, and experience will intensify their respective sexual identities from the moment they are born.

Hundreds of researchers have thus far failed to prove how much of the difference in the behavior of the two sexes has an organic source, how much of it is the result of social conditioning. In fact, scientists may never discover whether the psychological differences between the two are predominantly inborn, or chiefly a matter of training. But we can certainly hope to be enlightened about why the obvious sexual differences bring with them such characteristically dissimilar views on life and love.

One way to approach this intriguing question is to examine the way a child first becomes aware of the difference between masculine and feminine, and then begins to learn what will be expected of it as a boy or girl. With that established, it's possible to see how the experiences of adolescence and early adulthood underline and clarify these early lessons, until, as a full-fledged man or woman, the individual is facing life from a very different standpoint than

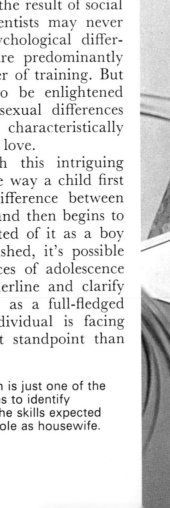

Helping Mommy in the kitchen is just one of the ways in which a little girl learns to identify with her mother, and acquire the skills expected of a woman in her traditional role as housewife.

Above: the most important man in a little girl's life is her father. The kind of relationship she enjoys with him will play a vital part in her developing attitude toward the opposite sex. A loving father can do much to help her make the transition from girlhood to womanhood.

Right: "Isn't she cute!" people say when they see a small girl dressed up in her Mommy's clothes or trying out her cosmetics. Little girls start imitating their mothers' behavior very early, and their efforts to look or be "just like Mommy" are usually met with indulgent smiles.

a member of the opposite sex would do.

Since we—both writer and reader—are women, it's naturally easiest to look at this inevitable development—and its effects on our lives—from an essentially feminine point of view. But because one of our main objectives is to gain some insight into what it's like to be the other half—with all the tribulations, as well as the liberties, that that entails—we'll also be trying to see things from the masculine point of view wherever possible. This will be especially true later on, when we get into the whole issue of a man's job and his affiliation with other men. We'll start, though, by taking a look at life, and the relation between the sexes, from an exclusively feminine point of view.

The very first man in a woman's life is her father. He enters the nursery rather late, and then he plays a very ambiguous role. He doesn't feed her, wash her, warm her or sing to her, and it is hard for her to be sure he even loves her with the same intensity that her mother constantly shows and proves. Oh yes, he cuddles her occasion-

ally, and he certainly isn't hostile. But he is always leaving. It is her mother who stays with her.

If a baby girl were to *think* (and she probably *feels*), what would she make of this large, genial creature who seems to be so absolutely useless when it comes to things like changing diapers? Is he some kind of big kewpie doll whose function will be clarified later on? For a long time, this father and the role he plays are a total mystery to her. Then gradually, as she grows in awareness, she realizes that he is connected to her and to her mother in some strong way, and that he is also their protector. It is daddy who links the family to the outside world and serves as a buttress against any threats that might come from that strange, vast place. It is daddy who drives the car and fixes things when they go wrong. It is daddy who provides for the family.

The little girl catches on to this last important fact fairly early, though probably never with the same impact as a caveman's child waiting for her father to bring home a tiger steak. Daddy's chief job it seems, is to be the provider. True, her mother may do the actual hunting in the supermarket, but it is her father who provides those odd bits of green paper necessary for buying the groceries. What is her father like in the big world where he gets those pieces of green paper? Daddy's life, between the closing of the front door behind him after breakfast and its opening again before dinner is an enigma. Her knowledge grows as she grows, but the enigma—the male mystique surrounding her father's life in the world outside—will never be completely cleared up for her.

If she has a brother, the little girl soon realizes that she is being treated differently from him, especially by their father. She is handled with more care than her brother, and discouraged from roughhousing, while he is not. Her punishments for disobedience are generally left to her mother, as though her father were somehow afraid

35

Within the family, special bonds tend to develop between mother and daughter, father and son. These bonds are reinforced by the behavior and activities traditionally assigned to each of the sexes, as girls and boys gradually learn to conform to the age-old patterns of sexual identity.

that she is more fragile than the boy. At times she may even notice that her father is worried about offending her with language that, she rightly guesses, he would not be so hesitant to use in the presence of his son. Gradually it becomes more and more clear to her that while her brother is meant to be toughened up, she is meant to be protected.

In terms of the relationships within the family, other differences begin to make themselves felt. Early in life, the little girl notices that her brother and her father have entered into a sort of contract within the family unit. Together they enjoy a unique form of comradeship, even complicity, from which both she and her mother seem to be excluded, however lovingly. It is as though, in some unexplained way, father and son are on the same wave length, and no matter how hard she tries, she can't tune in. She discovers, however, that she and her mother are on the same wave length. She notices that, if she tunes in—copies her mother's way of doing things, and forms the same bond of complicity with her that her brother has with her father—she will be winning approval by doing what is expected of her by both parents.

This is all part of the age-old pattern of teaching sexual identity. Boys, near the beginning of what is considered the normal course of events, are meant to identify with their fathers, who in turn are supposed to teach them how to be men. Girls are expected to identify with their mothers, and learn from them the complex art of being women.

Inside the family, the relating of son to

masculine and others feminine. Together, father and son will watch a football game on TV in the living room, for example, while mother and daughter retire to the kitchen to get dinner ready or wash the dishes. Later on, father and son will discuss mechanics or politics; mother and daughter will talk about clothes or the people they know. It is this unspoken but emphatic split within the family itself that is in large measure responsible for the endless passing on of both male and female behavior patterns from one generation to the next. It is also this early division of interests along the lines of sexual identity that helps to keep men and women such a mystery to one another from the very start.

Childhood games also play an important part in teaching a boy or girl what special traits he or she should develop (i.e., daring, courage, aggressiveness, if he's a boy; kindness, gentleness, modesty, if she's a girl). Generally speaking, boys are encouraged to vent their energies on the playground; girls are encouraged to tame theirs by quietly playing house and dressing their dolls. As a typical seven-year-old girl put it when asked to explain the difference between a boy and a girl: "A boy climbs trees, and a boy doesn't play with dolls. A boy doesn't play with girls." Girls, apparently, don't offer boys a sufficient challenge at this stage in their lives. That all comes later.

Little boys and girls take note of the physical differences between them surprisingly early. When they do, it is sometimes the little girls who feel (though such a feeling is not at all inevitable) that Nature has deprived them of an amusing ornament. The more frank and open the parents have been about sexual matters, the less disappointed a small girl is likely to feel about what appears to be her inadequacy. The fact remains, however, that in the beginning, she is physically distinguished from a boy by something she does *not* have, which can be a negative way of relating to her own body. Even after she has understood and

accepted the difference in the way she and her brother are made, a little girl may be left with the distinct feeling that there is more to this physical dissimilarity than meets the eye. Whatever else it may mean, she will soon learn that the way her brother is built is connected to the fact that he, and not she, will be initiated into the mysteries of her father's world.

Ask five little girls under seven what they want to be when they grow up and not one of them is likely to say an engineer, a bus driver, a dentist, a pilot, or whatever it is her father is. Four of them will say they want to be married, and the fifth might say that she wants to be married to an engineer, a bus driver, a dentist, a pilot, or whatever it is her father is. The father's occupation is a word without any real significance of its own. It is a synonym for father.

"My father is a doctor," or "My father is a salesman," simply means to the child that her father is a man and a man is a salesman or a doctor. For the same reason, five little boys under seven will tell you they want to be whatever it is their fathers are. "I want to be a Certified Public Accountant," one six-year-old boy said. "What does a Certified Public Accountant do?" "He drives a car and he doesn't eat lunch at home except on weekends."

Very early—child psychologists are saying a lot earlier than parents like to admit —a little girl learns how to flirt. While she is still a toddler, she discovers through observation and personal experience, that she can use her femininity to please, charm, and get her own way with members of the opposite sex. The first male on whom she tries out her feminine wiles is, of course, her father. Anyone who has watched a little girl with her father must know how early she learns how to use her feminine charms to establish a special relationship with a member of the opposite sex who is important to her.

Her early flirtation with her father is, in fact, her first lesson in making use of

Below: boy meets girl, toddler fashion. Very early, boys and girls discover the intriguing physical differences between them. How they react to this discovery depends a lot on how their parents answer their questions about sex.

Right: boy meets girl, teenage fashion. Now the emotional and sexual differences that made them strangers to each other as children form the basis of their mutual attraction as man and woman.

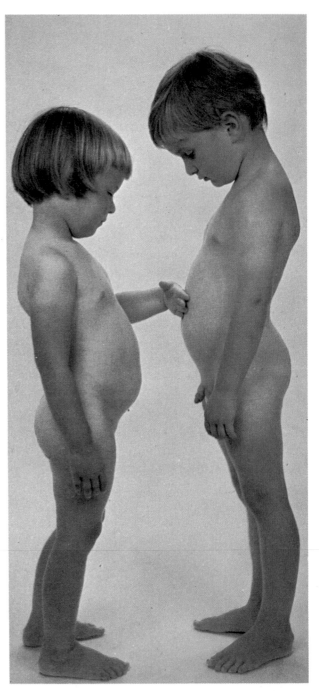

"Daddy's girl" soon discovers the joys of flirting with him. Fathers make ideal objects for little girls' first experiments in using their femininity to help them get their own way.

her sexual identity. Later on, this lesson will be further clarified and intensified as she discovers that it is her desirability as a female that gives her her real bargaining power in most of her relationships with men. All this is underlined by the fact that, unlike a boy, in whom vanity is traditionally scorned as effeminate, a girl is positively encouraged to spend her time, her allowance, and even to some extent her creativity, on becoming more and more an object of desire to the mysterious man who is to be her destiny.

Another difference in the way girls and boys learn the ultimate meaning of their sexual identity is that girls are impressed early with the dangers of sex—the chief one being an unwanted pregnancy. Most boys, although they have inhibitions and anxieties of their own, are usually aware much earlier of the pleasures of sex. Times are changing and sex education is narrowing the gap between the way adolescent boys and girls regard sex, but the daughters of most families are still raised to believe that it is unwise—even cheapening—to have sex before they are married, or at least before they have entered into some sort of steady relationship with a man they can love and depend on.

Girls are usually raised to believe that their purity and virginity has a special value, presumably in the marriage market, while for boys, virginity is considered unnecessary, even a disadvantage. While our society does not go so far as some in putting a price on a girl's virginity (in a few parts of the world today, it can be worth a whole herd of cattle in the marriage deal), we certainly do not encourage our daughters to have the same wide experience we expect our sons to have before marriage. Our views on the subject are nowhere near as strict as those of our Victorian grandparents, but it is still true that, while young men are given more or less carte blanche to play the field, young women are expected to save themselves for Mr. Right.

"He's fallen for her," we say of an infatuated male. "He's lost his head over her." This kind of remark points up the fact that sex is a woman's area of conquest in a far more direct and specific way than it is a man's. Our society holds the view that the ultimate prize for a woman is a male who is not her mother's, not her sister's, and preferably not her best friend's. According to the traditional ideal of romance, a woman's

Above: this late 19th-century painting illustrates the powerful role that flirtation has in a woman's relationships with men. The girl on the right, giving an unabashed display of her feminine charms, gets all the attention of the man, while the other girl is left to brood in a corner, alone and unnoticed.

Left: flirting is indeed a time-honored game between the sexes. Though it may not lead to anything more, it offers an easy and pleasant mode of communication between a man and a woman.

goal in this special arena of sexual conquest is a single, mysterious man of her own.

However much or long a young woman may hold out for this ultimate prize, she always knows that the easiest way to make contact with any man is to flirt with him. Flirting is a skillful and amusing activity that consists of presenting an enhanced, exaggerated, and somewhat fictional image of oneself to a member of the opposite sex. In a very real sense, flirting is like public relations. It does not promote genuine understanding; it arouses desire. When the flirting is over, more than one couple has discovered that they have absolutely nothing in common except perhaps, by that time, a mortgage, a car, and two kids.

Flirting, in fact, comes between men and women like a sheet of rose-colored glass that disguises the truth. Yet men like a woman to flirt, for it is in these terms that they are accustomed to seeing the female, and the flirt is therefore less alarming, less threatening, than a woman who thinks, a woman who competes, or a woman who is honest. Similarly, many women like to flirt because it places them in a comfortable, familiar orientation to the male, one in which they can be self-confident since experience has proven its efficacy.

Some women flirt with other women as well as with men, in an attempt to display only their most charming and disarming

Left: a cartoon view of the hapless male who's fallen for a woman's wiles and got caught in "the tender trap."

Right: the idealized image of romantic love has become something of a cliché. The handsome man and beautiful woman embracing in the glow of a golden sunset have more to do with Madison Avenue ads than with the realities of love and marriage.

characteristics. But most women tend to relax with members of their own sex, becoming caustic, earthy, silly, shrewd, witty, or whatever it is they really are. "When I'm married," said one young woman, surrounded by other women all in the various stages of having their hair done at a beauty salon, "I will never let my husband see me in curlers." This speaks volumes about the way women present themselves to one another, and the way they present themselves to the men in their lives. More telling than the fact they let members of their own sex see them with their hair down, women let other women see them with their hair up in curlers.

Yet, somehow, despite the flirting and the polished-up images of themselves that both men and women like to present to one another, love between the sexes goes on, and more or less happily, too. Although there is fear, fantasy, and misunderstanding on both sides, although even desire often wears odd disguises, men and women continue to attract, fascinate, need, depend on, often adore one another. Despite the frequently critical remarks they may make about their "better half," both men and women go on believing that, in certain indefinable ways, the opposite sex *is* better. "It's a funny thing," the head nurse at a maternity ward said in an interview. "Nine times out of ten, a first-time mother wants a son, but the fathers are different. I've seen men with real expressions of awe on their faces when they see their daughters for the first time. It's as if they were seeing an angel."

Mmmm, we may say, that's all very well when the girl is a baby, and a man's daughter to boot. But how does this reaction fit in with the whole complex of feelings he has had, does have, and will have toward the other women in his life —from his mother, sisters, and girlfriends, to the woman he has made his wife? How, in fact, do men really regard and relate to women?

The Making of a Man

3

However unsentimental men are supposed to be, they can be surprisingly tender-hearted. But the baby boy being cradled so gently by his dad will soon be subjected to a toughening-up process designed to discourage any qualities not consistent with the image of male strength.

Women are under scrutiny these days as never before. The so-called feminine mystique, the female sexual response, the issue of women's rights, the myriad problems of single girls, housebound wives, working mothers, career women, and divorcees, are all discussed, hotly and endlessly, in books, magazines, TV programs, even the movies. So much attention is being paid to female psychology, physiology, roles, and rights that one might almost think women were the inhabitants of a hitherto undiscovered continent.

Of men, of the husbands and fathers who have been running the world and, as some would have it, exploiting the women, for so long, we hear much less. This is not because there is less to tell. Nor is it because men don't

45

have problems. It is because male problems are not so obvious, not so easy to talk about, not even so easy to isolate and define. Nevertheless, they do exist, and could be said to be even more complex—because more deeply rooted in the question of sexual identity—than the problems facing women.

For centuries, men have complained— sometimes with bitterness, sometimes with affection, sometimes with secret relief—that their wives don't understand them. Even when they complain that their wives understand them too well, they only mean that their wives can see through them, or know how to manipulate men for their own ends. But men are usually right when they say their wives don't understand them, and there's a curiously universal reason why.

The fact is that both family structure and social fabric conspire to encourage a special kind of mystique around the male. Because it is traditionally the man, rather than the woman, who is expected to play the active role of pursuer, provider, and protector, it usually suits both parties to leave whatever inner conflicts he may have essentially undisturbed. It is as though the definition and analysis of his hangups would upset both the delicate balance between the sexes, and the whole set of assumptions on which society is based. Since men are ultimately in charge of things, it might prove a little unnerving to discover just how vulnerable, confused, and troubled they can actually be.

To know a man's problems is to know his weaknesses, and since both family and society are based on the special strengths men are supposed to possess, no one is especially eager to discuss (except in jokes and cliches) their real frailties and fallibilities as human beings. Even the most militant liberationists, for example—while berating women's status as the second sex, railing against the limitations that that status imposes on them, and campaigning for greater rights and freedoms —are unconsciously working within the age-old context of reliance on masculine strength and ability to take it. Men—like it or lump it —are at the helm. We expect them to be, and although we may ask them to change course somewhat and put right the injustices and inequalities that exist between the sexes, we expect them to be able to weather any storm and see us all safely into port.

That said, let's roll up our sleeves and take a look at one troubled area of masculine thinking that particularly affects us as women—namely, their role in the relations between the sexes. How do they see women, and why is their attitude toward love and sex so different from our own?

To begin with, boys are presented with a very contradictory picture of the opposite sex. They learn, very early, that girls are fragile, delicate, different. Little boys see that their sisters are treated with more gentleness, though not more love, by their parents, and particularly by their fathers. In some way, they realize, little girls are weaker than little boys and therefore—is it not logical?—in some way inferior, at least physically.

"Boys don't punch girls," they are told, and "Boys don't cry like girls do," and "Boys carry heavy books for girls; boys rescue girls' kittens out of trees; boys do not throw things or shout things at little girls." Little girls, it seems to a boy, are somehow more helpless and delicate than he is, and a careless little

boy might easily break one. Little girls, who cry, who can't throw balls or run as fast, whose sex is hidden, and who do "sissy" things such as playing with dolls and helping mother bake a cake, seem to need protection because they are weaker. (Of course, they can also be fun to tease, persecute, and exclude from the gang.)

All the time that a little boy is learning how little girls are more breakable, and less tough then he is, he is being looked after, scolded, and ordered around by a grown-up version of a little girl—his mother. The adult who, for the first few years of his life has absolute authority over his comings and goings, the person upon whom he is so dependent for food, love, and approval, the person to whom he must be obedient and respectful, the person who stays with him when his father goes away every morning, is a woman.

It is really not so surprising that, with these two conflicting images in his mind—that of the helpless little girl who needs protection, and that of the competent grown-up woman who has authority over him—a boy grows up never being quite sure what qualities to expect in a female. In most cases, the same

In childhood, boys and girls usually prefer the company of their own sex. Their different interests, physical capacities, and rate of development promote a form of sexual segregation, seen at its most pronounced on the playground. At this stage, they have only childhood in common.

confusion is not built into his idea of masculinity. His later assessment of himself, his father, his brothers, his friends, and his colleagues will be based on whether or not they possess the very qualities of daring, strength, and toughness he was encouraged to develop as a little boy.

If people went on behaving like children in this world, it is possible that men and women might never meet and mix. Both might continue to prefer the company of their own sex, feeling at home amid the familiar values and activities of their different worlds. If we went on being children, the pattern established in the family, at school, and on the playground—the pattern of separation by sex—would probably go right on, perhaps even as far as "his" and "hers" cemetaries, wherein would lie buried the future of mankind.

Fortunately for posterity, Nature is still more persuasive than custom, and, at a

49

For a small boy, looking after a little girl can be very trying. But what a difference ten years can make! His older brother, out with a girlfriend, is clearly making the most of his role as protective male.

certain age, little boys who have thus far avoided the boring company of little girls (who in turn have been avoiding the boorish company of little boys) discover the sexual attraction of the female. Suddenly, into the safe atmosphere of mutual segregation and slight contempt, into the tidy world divided by tree climbing and boys' clubs from doll houses and girls' clubs, suddenly sexual awareness has intruded, and nothing will ever be the same again.

This moment of discovery has, of course, been wildly overromanticized in a thousand different books and movies. (You know the scene: little boy stops stock still, blushes, stares, and stammers, as little girl next door passes by and it dawns on our young hero that She Is Something Special.) But over-romanticized or not, this moment of discovery is, in fact, the first of many moments in what is usually, for a boy, a period of acute agony—curiosity, interest, and the beginnings of desire, frustrated at every turn by shyness, inexperience, and the beginnings of feminine cruelty.

For a while, every young boy is Adam nibbling at the apple; it has more than poetic significance that the protuberance we call the Adam's apple appears at adolescence. Like Adam, the first fruits of this tree of knowledge turn his world upside down. Suddenly, he finds, he is no longer wholly his own master. Suddenly, a mere girl, one of those weak creatures he once regarded as inferior playmates, becomes a mysteriously attractive and desirable companion. This girl, by granting or withholding her approval, can make him happy or make him suffer . . . just as his mother did. Then comes the payoff—the full realization that his mother is a woman, just like this girl, and his father is a man, just like himself. The significance of this, in the light of his new sexual awareness, can be shattering to a boy. There has been no real research in this area, but it is not unlikely that girls, for all the problems that lie ahead, recover from the trials of puberty faster than boys, many of whom never really seem to recover at all.

Below: one of the chief factors in a man's choice of wife is the sheer availability of a suitable partner. No man has all the world to pick from; various circumstances filter out all but a handful of possibilities, as this chart clearly demonstrates. Below right: once the choice has been narrowed down to a few, a man has the enjoyable task of making his final selection.

Most young men are taught, no matter how subtle the teaching, that purity is the greatest female virtue. Sexual awareness disturbs the whole balance of his knowledge of women. Purity may be the apex of feminine virtue, but how he longs to find a loving female who is not quite so virtuous, or who will stop being perfectly virtuous for him. His future wife must be very pure and faithful, but right now he wants to make love to every pretty girl he meets, even the one he might one day wish to marry. A young man's sexuality is not notably discriminating, but he desperately wants some guidelines about

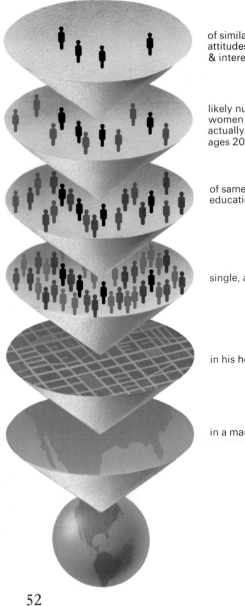

of similar intelligence, attitudes, values, & interests

likely number of these women a man will actually meet between ages 20-29

of same social class & educational standard

single, aged 20

in his home town or city

in a man's own country

where to direct it. Faced with this puzzling array of female creatures—these perplexing objects of desire and respect, these weaklings who can dominate a man's life, these mystifying women who say they want just one man but who do their best to attract as many as possible—he finds that the easiest way to sort them out is to classify and categorize them. To make things easier still, he finds that there is a whole range of categories already drawn up for him—from "sex kitten" to "girl next door," from "clinging vine" to "career woman," from "with-it chick" to "home-loving little mother."

A leading woman's magazine—one of those whose chief aim seems to be to perpetuate the age-old cliches about both men *and* women—recently asked 40 celebrated bachelors to describe their ideal woman. Here is a sampling of their answers: "A good cook and good looking . . . faithful, too." "Someone who constantly looks glamourous." "Plenty of drive, but in the end, likes to be dominated." "Charm, understanding, a liberal outlook, and above all, the ability to give you that indefinable feeling of excitement each time you see her." "Give me a wholesome, well-made female any day."

For most men, a vital ingredient of "the good life" is home and family. In fact, for many men, real happiness only begins when they find a loving, understanding wife and start having children of their own to raise and be proud of.

"I'd prefer a home-type to an out-and-out career girl."

Notice that most of these ideal women not only fit into one or another of the categories listed earlier, but also represent some kind of fantasy figure that meets the particular man's needs to a tee, and makes no special demands of her own. It is interesting, too, that not one of the men interviewed mentioned honesty as an attribute of his ideal woman, though that quality would probably be high on his list of priorities for a male friend. Whatever it is a man looks for in a woman, the historical separation of the sexes in the home and in the world at large has not led him to expect from her the same kind of forthrightness, challenge, and camaraderie he looks for in a man.

These men were describing fantasy women, though, and how can a fantasy be honest? The moment authenticity walks in, fantasy walks out, and evaporates into thin air. Women are well aware of this and, like the moguls of advertising and the media, spend a good deal of time, energy, and money encouraging men to go on believing in their fantasies. The more like a man's dream-creature she is, the more likely a woman is to be chosen as his wife. For this reason, women are only too willing to break their backs, their bank accounts, and their fattening habits to fill the bill. For this reason, too, women tend to suppress the special qualities of mind and heart that make each of them unique. They're afraid of *not* fitting neatly into a category. When a man says to a woman, "You're different," she does not always know whether he means it as a compliment or a criticism. He probably doesn't know either, but it adds a disturbing

element of uncertainty to their relationship. If 18 melons are sitting on a shelf and only one of them is pink, it will take a rare buyer to choose the odd one—even though it may be a delicious new variety.

Recently, more and more men have been forced to take a closer look at women, to see the complex individuals behind the pretty masks. Sometimes the reaction is shocked surprise, sometimes genuine admiration and pleasure. But a great many women still refuse to be seen without their psychological make-up on. A great many more refuse to look closely at the men in their lives, at the mysterious, hard-working, complicated men they're married to. Possibly, in the same way that some men are afraid to find strength and independence in their wives, many women are afraid to find weakness and self-doubt in their husbands. Both sexes tend to shy away from an honest confrontation with each other as human beings.

Until the day when this kind of confrontation is not only possible, but genuinely desired, both sexes will go on being mystified about the other and their relations with the other. Perhaps in some ways it is more difficult for men to keep their footing in this realm these days than it is for women, who have begun to find their feet and make rapid strides in the direction of self-awareness.

Men find their role increasingly difficult to define, especially nowadays when the women in their lives—once so easily organized into stereotypes and categories—have developed such a disconcerting way of blossoming into real people. The one girl in the office who could be depended on for her neatness, tact, and efficiency suddenly

announces that she's pregnant and her boy-friend has left her. The sexy starlet admired from afar for her womanly curves and her ultra-femininity, leaves the movies to start campaigning all over the world for the rights of underprivileged minorities. A man's own wife, who for years has seemed content with her role as devoted wife and mother, turns around one day and tells him she's fed up with staying at home and is going out to get a job. And possibly most disturbing of all, his pretty teenage daughter, the girl-child he's been breaking his back to send through college, up and tells him she's dropping out of school to hitch-hike to Mexico, so she can "see what life's *really* all about."

It is no native selfishness that has taught men to want the impossible; they have done it with the encouragement of women who seemed to promise the impossible. There was the little girl next door, the fragile blonde who, when he finally screwed up his courage and asked her out, turned into a tease and laughed at him in front of his friends. There were all the false eyelashes he mistook for real ones, there were all the females who melted with loving sex and then made unloving demands, there were all the women who gave him their bodies and then made him feel guilty. There was always the perfect im-possibility of fact and fantasy living inside "36-24-36", there was always the confusion of women giving him authority and then objecting when he used it. Above all, under all, over all, there was the sex act, ideally a moment of love, but in fact a perilous mo-ment, a moment when he risked—and always risks—humiliation and weakness be-fore a woman.

Is it any wonder that men sometimes tend to see their jobs as a refuge, and retreat with a certain amount of relish from the whole sexual turmoil into the relatively safe world of business? There, whatever the challenges, the pressures, and the competition, they are in the company of people they really understand, and in turn are understood by—other men.

It has been said that a man looks to different women to fulfill different needs in his life. Here we have what might be a man's ideal cast of female characters: adoring daughter, loving wife, doting mother, admiring secretary, sexy mistress. With such a collection of ego-building females around him, a man could hardly fail to feel as pleased with himself as the lucky fellow in our photograph. Of course, life isn't alto-gether like that, as most men know only too well.

56

A Man and His Job

4

Men at work. In many ways, a man's job is the most important factor in his life. Whatever he does for a living, his work becomes a vital part of his self-definition as a man. Eight hours a day, five days a week—and sometimes more—he is proving his worth in a competitive world where demands are great and the pressure rarely lets up.

"Man does; woman is." This is how one would-be wit once summed up the difference between the sexes. Of course, it's simplistic—any statement like this usually is. But it does point up one aspect of the difference that we all acknowledge, consciously or unconsciously: that while a woman is usually measured in terms of what she *is*—her looks, her personality, and especially her marital status—a man is usually measured, first and foremost, in terms of what he *does*—his job and how successful he is at it.

Think about it for a minute. If you were stopped in the street by an interviewer, and asked to state in a single sentence the most important factor in your daily life, you'd probably say, "My family—my husband and children." Asked the same question, however, a man would probably say: "My job," and then state what it is.

This is not because a man's family is unimportant to him—far from it. It's more because the chief focus of a man's energies, and the realm in which he is expected to prove himself, lies outside the home, while a woman's (unless she is single) lies inside it. In a sense, too, it's a question of traditional priorities. Our culture is essentially built around the idea that it is a woman's role to marry and have children, while it is a man's to enter a trade, profession, or business in order to support himself and his family. It is still true that the first question we usually ask about a woman is, "Married or single?" while the first question we ask about a man is, "What does he do for a living?" Though

59

GETS FEDERAL
CONTRACT

FIXES MERGER
WITH THE
COMPETITION

FOUND ASLEEP
ON THE JOB

MISBEHAVES
AT CHRISTMAS
PARTY

MARRIES BOSS'S
DAUGHTER

GETS INTO MANAGEMENT
TRAINING COURSE

A humorous view of one man's journey up the ladder of success. But, as most men know, getting to the top is usually a grim and serious business.

a woman, too, must work if she's single, it is usually a matter of choice whether she does or not after she's married. But a man must always work, married or single, if he is to keep his pride.

Today, more and more women are proving their competence and finding their fulfillment in the once exclusively masculine domains of business and the professions. This does not mean that more and more men are proving their competence and finding their fulfillment in the feminine domains of housekeeping and child rearing. What it means is that, increasingly, women have two possible avenues of achievement open to them—home and work—while men continue to have only one—work. The full significance of what a man's work means to him must never be underestimated.

From the time he is small, a boy is persistently asked, "What do you want to be when you grow up?" At first, of course, his answer will probably be, "an electrician," "a doctor," "a taxi driver," "a businessman," or whatever it is his father is. But everywhere in this land of opportunity of ours it has become a basic belief that a son should try not only to equal, but also to go beyond his father's achievement. So he will be encouraged to aim higher than his dad. The field in which he must excel may be the same, but he is expected to do better, to get higher up the ladder of success. Thus, the construction worker may want his son to be a building contractor, the accountant may want his son to be a management consultant, the general practitioner may want his son to be a heart specialist. Just as often, the boy is encouraged to excel by doing something altogether different from his dad—to become a white collar worker instead of a blue collar worker, for example, or to enter medicine or the law rather than going into business. But whether the field is the same or different, the basic expectation is, in almost every case, that the son will gain more status and make more money than his dad. Unlike the Far East and many parts of Europe, where boys automatically step into their fathers' pro-

Fathers are often ambitious for their sons, cherishing the hope that their boys' achievements will not only equal, but surpass, their own. For a man, a son's success is not only a source of pride in itself, but also an extended fulfillment of his own dreams.

Left: a pint-sized version of "winner take all." Whether in an organized meet or in a casual back lot game, boys feel the pressure to prove their athletic prowess. From an early age, competitive sports form an integral part of male rivalry.

Right: to the victor belong the spoils—in this case, a fast car and a pretty girl. The outward symbols of success can make a man the envy of his friends and enhance his own self-image. But a man needs more than status symbols to give his life meaning.

fessional shoes and thus maintain the family position, the American male is expected to fill professional shoes three sizes larger than his dad's. The pressure this can place on a man can be enormous, sometimes crushing. Imagine that society expected you to prove that you were a more understanding wife, a more loving and patient mother, a more efficient housekeeper, a wiser budgeter, or a better cook than your own mother ever was. Then you can get some idea of the kind of psychological burden most men carry.

This upward mobility syndrome, in which a boy is, in a sense, in competition with his own father, is but another aspect of the competitive spirit that permeates his whole experience of growing up. He learns the rudiments of this competitiveness in the aggressive games he plays with other boys

on the playground; in the hand-to-hand, do-or-die combats he cannot avoid with the bullies in his neighborhood; in the drinking contests and sexual bragging sessions ("How far did you get with her?") of his later adolescence; in the pressure to get good grades so that he can get into a university, college, or professional school; in the battle to get the kind of job his training has prepared him for.

Once he has that job, the competitiveness never lets up. To keep his job or move on to a better one, to get raises and promotions, he must keep on proving that he is as good at it —and preferably better at it—than the next man. His job becomes the measure of his own manhood, not only in his eyes, but in the eyes of his friends, colleagues, wife, and family.

"I knew he was going places when I

married him," said the wife of a well-known politician in a recent interview. "We always had faith in him," said the mother of a self-made millionaire, "We knew he would accomplish whatever he set out to do."

Ambition, that much-prized virtue of the American male, is encouraged and admired in every field. It lends a special aura of value to the man who possesses it, as though he were somehow better, more self-confident, more born to succeed than the man who is content to remain at a certain level in his field. But equally, ambition may be a sign that a man lacks confidence in his ultimate worth, that he feels driven to prove his value by the outward symbols of success.

The man who is happy to level off at a certain rung in the ladder of success may be a trial to his wife. ("I just don't know what's the matter with Bob; I keep telling him he could do better. I know he could get a promotion if he'd only play his cards right, but he just won't make the effort.") The man in question, however, may not really want a promotion. More money, yes; more head-aches, no. He may already have realized the kind of losses that such a gain might entail. As one man, recently promoted from the ranks, put it, "I don't really enjoy the new job. I used to be just one of the guys. Now I'm in charge of them and responsible for the work they do. It's sort of lonely. I can't talk to them the way I used to, and besides, it means putting in a lot more hours than I did before. I'm physically and mentally bushed when I get home."

If a man is going to be less happy with more responsibility, if it means he's going to have less peace of mind, and less time and energy for the other things in life he enjoys, a wise wife will accept his leveling off, and love her man for the way he is. This is all the more true if one of his chief reasons for not driving himself is that he values his home life. Any man who instinctively resents the idea of robbing Peter to pay Paul, i.e., getting ahead in his job at the expense of losing touch with his family, is worth his weight in gold. All-or-nothing ambition can do drastic things to a man's role as husband and father.

"His work," said one unhappy woman suing for divorce, "is the other woman. Sometimes I wish it really had been somebody else, some blonde from the office. That would have been much easier to fight. But how do you compete with a growing chain of TV repair shops? It's impossible. A lot of women might think I'm silly for not just buying diamonds and minks. I might have thought so once, too, but now I know what I want is a husband who's there. He has the touch for business, that's true. We worked together for the first shop and those were really happy days. But now he can't stop. He says it's for me and the kids, but his out-of-town contacts see more of him than I do, and the kids never ask him to affairs at their school any more. They know he'll be too busy to come, and they feel hurt by his refusal".

"He works 80 hours a week," said the admiring campaign staff of a politician, and everyone who read the article was impressed. But a week holds only 168 hours, and if the man works 80 hours and sleeps, say, a minimum of 42 hours, his family is

Above: working late in the office, long after everyone else has gone home, can be pretty lonely. But driving ambition is a hard task-master, and the man determined to succeed often finds he has to sacrifice much of his home life to the demands of his business career.

Left: the children of the man who regularly works late have to get used to not seeing daddy before they go to bed.

seeing less of him than his staff. In fact, many men, in various fields, find that as their success increases, and the pace of their career accelerates, they spend less and less time at home. They are doing what men are encouraged to do—being ambitious and taking on more and more responsibility—but in the process, they are losing touch with their wives and children.

And losing touch can mean more than a husband's spending fewer hours at home. Many a wife has discovered that her husband, exposed to a greater variety of influences in the world of business than she may be in the relatively limited world of home and family, has undergone a fundamental change in outlook, one that makes him more at ease in certain social situations than she is. One woman, for example, bemoaning the ever-widening gap between her own and her husband's sophistication, described the acute sense of discomfort she felt at a dinner party with his high-powered business associates. "All those rich and important friends made me so shy and nervous that I just sat in a corner and got quietly drunk. When I married him we lived in one room and ate spaghetti four times a week. Do you know, I remembered those days with longing!"

Whether or not a man's job takes him onward and upward into realms where his wife feels at a disadvantage, his job usually becomes a part of him in a way that she cannot fully understand. Even if he dislikes the company he works for, even if he dislikes the particular work he does, his job comes to have a meaning for him that goes beyond the mere necessity of earning money. Of course, it is the means by which he supports himself and his family, pays the bills and meets the installments on the car, the mortgage, and the life insurance policy. Of course, too, it is the means through which he gives expression to his own particular talents and abilities. But, in a very real sense, though he probably sees his work as a means to these and other specific ends, his job is an end in itself. It is there that he focuses his energies, there that he finds a sense of purpose, direction, and continuity, there that he feels himself truly a man among men.

Though women are slowly—very slowly —beginning to infiltrate the ranks of commerce and industry, politics and the professions, these realms are still very much dominated by men. It is no wonder that men want to keep it that way. Work is the one place where they can escape the complications, misunderstandings, and bewilderments that often arise in their relationships with women. Work is the one place where their role is clearly defined and their masculinity emphatically reinforced. At work they give and take orders, meet challenges, and wage battles with people whose motivations, objectives, and basic viewpoints they share—other men. These are individuals they understand. This is a context in which they feel they themselves will be understood, and in which they can operate with greater confidence, freedom, and efficiency than in the realm of male-female relationships.

In fact, many men really function best at work. "I'll never forget the day my father took me to visit the workroom in his garment factory," one New York writer reminisced. "There he became a man I had never met before, a man of humor and stature and power. Why, he seemed to grow as we entered the door. But what had happened to the small man who put his false teeth in a glass every night? Where was that weakling my mother was forever saying she gave up the best chances of her life for? Gone! And in his place stood this captain of industry. I even remember that on his desk was an ashtray. At home he never smoked."

Few women appreciate—because they

A Day in the Life...

In an average working day, the modern urban man sees surprisingly little of his family. If he gets a good night's sleep, does a full day's work, and, like most men these days, has to spend a couple of hours getting to and from his job, he ends up having only a few hours a day to enjoy the company of his wife and children.

8 hours' sleep

1 hour breakfast and getting dressed

1 hour traveling

9 hours at work (including lunch)

1 hour traveling

4 hours' leisure time

rarely see it—the subtle transformation a man undergoes when he leaves behind him the complexities of his personal life and steps into the relatively straightforward world he works in. Before him lies the simple challenge of doing his job. If few women realize how satisfying the simplicity of that single challenge can be, it's an even rarer woman who can fully understand that, for long periods each day, her husband's job must be more important to him than she is. Her picture may be in his wallet, but when he is working on an assembly line, driving a taxi, examining patients, or making executive decisions, thoughts of her are far from him. She works in surroundings permeated by his presence, but he really does leave her every morning when he goes off to work.

Michael Korda, author of an article in *Glamour* magazine called "Sexual Politics in the Office," really spares no punches in describing what he thinks the office really means to the American male. (And surprisingly enough, it is not flirting with the office sex kitten—quite the reverse, in fact.) He says: "Office life is neither a test of modified prehistoric skills, nor the rationally conducted activity we like to pretend it is, but a self-perpetuated masculine myth, whose basic impulse is *precisely to escape from women.*"

Korda goes on to say that "men have succeeded in institutionalizing their work and transforming the unfortunate necessity of earning a living to support themselves and the families that *they* have created (nobody obliged them to marry or have children) into an escapist ritual as powerful

There was a time when a man's work was more closely integrated with his family life than it is today. As these pictures show, husband and wife worked together to accomplish many of the tasks on which their livelihood depended. Of course, this was especially true of such traditional agricultural labors as reaping, gathering fruit, and sheepshearing. But even in the field of moneylending (an early form of banking), it was common for wives to help their husbands.

69

as the warrior rites of any primitive tribe. There is no togetherness in America to match the togetherness of men at work. . . . When women enter this world and try to compete in it, they are in effect penetrating a mystery, defiling a temple, for the myth of the modern American man is not sex, or family, or democracy, but *work*. It is at work that he feels most at ease, in a world that he and his peers have created in their own image."

That's pretty strong stuff, but there's probably more than a grain of truth in it. Still, the world of "chummy masculinity"— as Korda describes it—can be anything but comfortable for the men who inhabit it. Mistakes are easy to make, pitfalls often difficult to avoid. Most men have a step in front of them that they want to climb, or that their wives are nagging them to climb—to be foreman, manager, or to own their own business. Almost every man with a job has someone behind him, someone younger, with more advanced or recent training, who wants what he has. Nowadays, the heaviest pressures on a working man are psychological ones: the pressure to do his job well, the pressure to be seen doing his job well, the pressure to be promoted, the pressure to please his boss without

Above: the miseries of getting to and from work add greatly to the stresses of a man's working day. The ordeal of fighting his way through subway crowds or traffic jams may leave him feeling utterly exhausted by the time he reaches home.

Right: a man's home can be a welcome refuge after a hard day's work. This is all the more true if he has learned to leave his work problems behind him, and can relax with his wife and children in a tension-free atmosphere.

demeaning himself, the pressure to make himself indispensable.

An employer and his employee do not exchange rings and vows; they can leave each other quite easily—and abruptly. The fruits of a man's labors, moreover, are no longer a crop of wheat or a freshly killed bear, but just an impersonal pay check, most of which goes to pay the bills and buy the groceries. This pay check, this impersonal product of his labors, gets turned over, whole or in part, to his wife, who has more and more trouble stretching it, and who, quite logically, may sometimes ask why he can't make more. It is no wonder that the modern man after his day's work is just as tired as the old-time wheat-thresher or big game hunter used to be.

"When did it start happening?" said one man, a sales manager for a toy firm. "It was probably after the two kids were born. The fun went out of everything at home. I know it isn't easy for her to manage, but when I get home after a day in the office, I just can't help her. The minute I walk across the threshold, I just fold up. I mean, all the pressures of the day sort of collapse inside me and all I want is a drink, a bite to eat, and nothing to do. She gets upset because I don't help out. I don't blame her,

Every man has days when he feels overwhelmed by his problems. Prices are soaring, the house may need repairs, and perhaps he's failed to get a promotion he was counting on. He may also feel alienated from his children, and depressed by the onset of his own middle age. It is at such moments that he most needs his wife's love and willingness to share his doubts and worries.

but how can I explain that the boss has been on my back all day about an order that was returned. She says I have it easy, she doesn't even have Sunday off, but the truth is, sometimes on Sunday night when I look at a whole week of problems ahead of me, I really don't know how I'm going to get through it."

Possibly, this man has made the mistake that Michael Korda says all too many men do: "They have voluntarily placed their deepest emotions in their work, given their soul to the corporation without the corporation even asking for it, made a specific task into a ritual—hence the familiar spectacle of the man who puts so much of himself into his job (he may not be working hard, but he's giving *himself*) that his marriage founders because he isn't home, or when he is home he's too tired to be of any use as a husband and father."

It's a familiar spectacle, as Korda says, and, of course, it's the wife who usually bears the brunt of it. It's a state of affairs that can happen all too easily, at least at present. It's a kind of trap. Our society encourages us to see a man's job as the symbol of his worth, even of his virility, and so, unfortunately, a man may use himself up chasing the great American dream of success, leaving nothing for the things which could bring him an even deeper source of satisfaction—his relationships with his wife and children.

Perhaps the worst hazard of this emphasis on a man's job is the possibility that he might lose it. Nothing, we say, succeeds like success, but what we don't like to add is that nothing fails like failure. As a man's success is measured largely by his progress at work, and thus by the house he lives in, the car he drives, and the way he supports his family, so his failure is often measured in the same way. Though his wife and family ought essentially to have other and more loving measures of his success as a husband, a father, and a man, they, too, are under the acquisitive pressures of modern life, and sometimes tend to see him chiefly in terms of his success as a provider.

It's painful to admit it, but only a minority of wives are genuinely interested in their husbands' work. Many cannot even describe precisely what it is their husbands spend most of the week doing. Far less do they understand how much a job means to a man in terms of his self-esteem.

When a man loses his job, especially if he is an older man, his world crumbles around him. The only way for a woman to appreciate such a disaster in a man's life is to imagine how she would feel if she went to the store for groceries and came back to find a gaping hole where her home had been. When a man loses his job, when he faces this gaping hole in his life, he may think—and often he is right in thinking so—that his wife and children do not fully appreciate what this means to him as a man. It may suddenly strike him that his wife and children are not really dependent upon *him*, but upon his job and pay check —not the same thing at all.

That men and women can grow so detached within their marital roles, and see each other so one-dimensionally despite the length of time they have spent together, is suggested by the startling fact that many men who have been fired or laid off prefer to carry on for months as though nothing had happened, rather than tell their families the truth. Just as often, their families, the people who should know them better than anyone else does, never even guess that something has gone wrong.

"I left home at the usual time," says one man who was laid off in his mid-40's, "and at the usual time I came home. I'd spend the days looking for work at first, but then I just went to sit in the park if the weather was good. I used to give my wife cash for the housekeeping and, what with savings and unemployment benefits, I managed to keep it up. I just couldn't bring myself to tell her. How do you tell your family you're not a man anymore? You'd be surprised, too; in the park on those afternoons I met other guys just like me."

When a man does bring himself to tell his wife what has befallen him, it can be the making or the breaking of their relationship. It's chiefly up to her. She must be prepared, without any exhibition of self-sacrifice, to go out and get a job if that is necessary to tide them over until he is on his feet again. She must be ready, without any signs of pity for him, to listen to his explanation of what happened, and his problems in finding another job. She must be able, without being ostentatious about it, to break out of the role she has played up to now, the role of the dependent, and take up the role of an equal partner in the marriage.

The loss of a job can be the beginning of a new depth in the relationship between a husband and his wife. When the chips are down, a man's best friend can, and should, be his wife. As she should be able to turn to him in times of trouble, so he should be able to turn to her—and without any loss of face. In the end, this is what marriage is all about—a mutual commitment to one another as people, and a readiness to share whatever life may bring— and that means the bad with the good.

Below: when a man loses his job, he may take it as a sign of utter failure. If he cannot bring himself to talk about it, he may withdraw into a mood of loneliness and despair.

Below right: the loss of a job need not be a problem that a man has to face all alone. In fact, if he feels free to discuss it fully with his wife, this kind of upheaval in a man's working life can be the beginning of a renewed sense of partnership and understanding between them.

A Man and His Friends 5

One of the most common causes of friction and misunderstanding between husbands and wives is extramarital friendships—his, not hers. No, we are not talking about other women, we're talking about his pals, his buddies, the guys he drinks with, plays poker with, goes to baseball or football games with, etc. The mere phrase "a night out with the boys," often uttered with obvious glee by a man, may just as often produce an inward groan on the part of his wife. This despite the fact that she may know perfectly well that he's not going to get into any real mischief while he's out. It's the relish with which he looks forward to these get-togethers with his friends that may annoy, even hurt her. Why should he want to get out of the house when he's out of the house most of the week anyway? Why should he need these friends when he's got her and the children?

It's very simple, really. These friends provide him with the same comforting re-assurance of his masculine identity that his job does—and sometimes better than his job does. At work there are pressures, sometimes very heavy pressures, and he may occasionally feel that he is just another cog in the wheel, unappreciated except in terms of what he can do, and how well he can do it. At home, too, there are pressures—subtle, or not-so-subtle problems with his wife, a growing sense of alienation from his children, difficulties with his in-laws, etc. But with his friends, he's accepted for what he is, and the tensions and responsibilities of family life recede into the background. With his friends, he gets all the chummy masculinity—that sharing of comfortably male assumptions about sex, money, sport, and politics—that he enjoys at work,

Liberty, equality, fraternity—that's what friendship means to a man. When he's out with his pals, a man's problems and responsibilities seem to melt away, and he feels free to relax and enjoy himself. With his friends, he shares easy-going camaraderie and solidarity that boost his male ego and make him feel ready to take on the world.

In many countries, it's considered perfectly natural for men to express their regard for their friends by greeting them with a hug or strolling along arm in arm with them. In our society, however, such spontaneous gestures of friendship are only permitted in childhood.

without any of the specific pressures that can make his working life so hard.

This is not to say that a certain amount of competitiveness isn't part and parcel of his friendships with other men. Bred in a spirit of competition with other males, a man usually feels a certain pressure to prove himself—with his friends no less than with his work mates. Since strength and toughness, skill and daring, virility and self-confidence are all highly prized male attributess, most men try to impress their friends by showing off these qualities. A man and his friends are not rivals in earnest, but there is something at stake, something they feel bound to go on proving: their masculinity.

This friendly rivalry, this competition between or among friends, can take many forms—from how well a man can hold his liquor to how good he is at touch football, from how pretty or easy-going his wife is to whether or not he's going places at work, from what kind of a car he has to how much he's improved the value of his house, from how much action he saw in the war to how many women he's had, from how many times he's been stopped for speeding to how good a card player he is, from how well his kids are doing at school to where he takes the family on their vacations.

Always, however—or, at least, in 99 cases out of 100—the friendship, and the competitive spirit that enlivens it, is carried on between equals or near equals. A man and his friends will be about the same age, for example. It's more rare to see men of vastly differing age groups bound in friendship than it is to see May-December marriages. Sexual attraction seems to be able to leap barriers that friendship finds more difficult to surmount. A man and his friends are also usually in the same income bracket, and may even be in the same field. "Talking shop" comes as naturally to men as "talking babies" does to women. And finally, a man and his friends usually share the same kind of background, the same kind of lifestyle, and the same kind of goals in terms of what they want in the future.

Much of this could be said about friendships between women as well. Most of a woman's friends, for example, will be about her age, have the same marital status, and, if married, have children about the same age as her own. They will probably also come from a background similar to her own, live in much the same way as she does, and have the same general expectations of life.

Young bachelors do most of their girl-hunting in packs. The support and encouragement of his friends bolsters a young man's confidence and sharpens his roving eye. It's not hard to imagine the kind of remarks these girls are inspiring among the threesome ogling them. ·

Also (need we say it?) friendships between women, like friendships between men, usually contain an element of competition. It might be about how well they keep their looks, or how well they keep their houses, or how well they manage on their husband's salary, or how healthy, handsome, or good their children are. Who has not heard a woman say, with a certain smug satisfaction, "My baby was completely toilet-trained by the age of 12 months." Or, "I can still get into the dress I wore at my engagement party. I haven't put on an ounce since then." Women, even when they are the best of friends, are always ever so slightly in competition with one another, feeling pride or envy, for example, at how well their respective husbands are doing, or how loving, helpful, or attentive those husbands are. The difference is that women are less open about their competitiveness than men are. Whatever rivalry they feel, whatever boasting they do, takes a far subtler form than a man's.

Often, when two male friends meet each other, they greet each other with punches and mild blows. Any Martian seeing this phenomenon for the first time, might take these gestures as a sign of aggression. In fact, they symbolize the sort of rough, tough, hearty and hard-bitten manliness that every man likes to believe he possesses. (They are also, incidentally, the only ways in which men can show their affection for each other. In our society, hugging is strictly for women.) It is certainly true that one of the chief satisfactions a man gets from his friendships is this reinforcement of his masculine image.

Inside many a gentle husband and steady job holder is a Hemingway hero dying for a

chance to prove himself in hand-to-hand combat, to spear killer sharks, to drink everyone else under the table with no hangover the next day, and to leave a trail of heart-broken beauties in every port. Of course, what usually happens in life is that he rarely sees any more action than swearing at the driver in front of him, gets fat from drinking beer, loses at pinochle, catches a bad cold in the bleachers, and takes an occasional side-long glance at the sweater girl in the typing pool. But however mild the man, however humdrum his existence, he may feel that deep

When men get together, it's usually to *do* something—a shared hobby or activity —and it's usually outside the home. Whether it's fishing, studying, golfing, drinking, or just watching the world go by, a man's interest or pastime takes on a special value if shared with other men.

within him lie untapped reserves of strength and daring. It is this fantasy of himself that his man-to-man friendships reinforce.

Many of the ideal qualities of male friendships are formed in the army, or, for those who escape military service, in the very idea of the army. When men work together in an exclusively male community and, theoretically at least, depend upon each other for life itself, the resulting relationships are something more than ordinary friendships based on shared interests. The standards of this high and rare relationship between fighting men have become a sort of touchstone for even the most peaceful friendships. These standards of honor and courage in the face of an enemy exclude women altogether. Not that women cannot fight—they can, like tigresses, when cornered, or when their loved ones are threatened. But women are not taught to enjoy a good fight, or to seek ways of proving their strength and courage. They haven't been brought up on the fictional heroes who risk their lives to pull wounded buddies out of the front line, or stand shoulder to shoulder with a friend in time of danger. Men have,

and a certain element of this romantic notion of shared danger can creep into any relationship between men. Big businessmen may see each other as blood brothers in the dog-eat-dog world of high finance, like soldiers together on the firing line. Workers on the factory floor may see themselves as blood brothers in the continuing struggle against management, back-to-back, battling the bosses.

Women are often puzzled by the seeming unreality of this element in male friendships. ("A friend is someone you can trust in a

Women have never found it very easy to accept the idea that their menfolk sometimes prefer "a night out with the boys" to an evening at home with the family.

Above: cards, cash, beer, and cigars—add a handful of men, and you have all the necessary ingredients for that typically masculine idea of a perfect evening—a poker game.

Left: this humorous depiction of a scene in the smoking room of a 19th-century men's club epitomizes the enduring male need for a temporary escape from the realm of women, into a world where all the doors read "Men Only."

tight situation," says a shoe salesman whose wife knows perfectly well that the tightest situation he's been in for 20 years has been the belt of his trousers.) But men are very sensitive to signs of bravery and courage in each other, however unlikely it may be that they will be called upon to prove them. On the whole, this is a rather endearing aspect of male friendships.

Of course, this ability to count on a guy usually boils down to something less heroic than meeting physical challenges together. On a realistic level, friendships between men have a great deal in common with friendships between women. Both sexes place a high value on friendship, and look for essentially the same things in a friend: loyalty, for example, and mutual support, sympathy and understanding, and a willingness to help out when the going gets rough. A friend, for either sex, is someone you like and trust, someone you can laugh with, talk with, relax with, be yourself with. A friend is also someone you can see fairly often, and with whom you have enough in common to confide in, share information with, or seek advice from.

It is interesting that happily married couples tend to have more joint friends than unhappily married couples. It is also interesting that couples with the largest number of friends seem to have both the greatest number of mutual friends and the greatest number of

The traditionally masculine virtues of honor, fortitude, and bravery in the face of danger have often found their highest expression in the comradeship of men in war. Perhaps this is why the element of "do-or-die" loyalty plays a basic part in most male friendships. Far left: playing soldiers has always been a favorite boy's game. Left: army cadets on parade at West Point. Below: war veterans meet to reminisce about past glories.

separate friends. What this indicates is that the capacity for making and keeping friends is closely tied to the very qualities that make for a happy marriage, qualities such as openness and loyalty, tolerance and dependability.

Perhaps the one major difference between male and female friendships is that men get together primarily for the purpose of doing something, while women meet chiefly to talk. It is here that a certain amount of marital discord can rear its ugly head. For while women usually meet to talk in one another's homes, men, when they meet to do something together, often meet outside one another's

Exclusive societies, rich in secrecy and symbolism, have always had a strong appeal for men. Perhaps the best known is the society of Freemasons, founded in the 17th century as a revival of the stonemasons' guilds of the Middle Ages. Left: ritual ceremonies have played a vital role in Freemasonry from its earliest beginnings. Below left: a modern Freemason candidate undergoes an elaborate initiation ceremony. Tradition requires that, blindfolded, and with his chest and one leg bared, he be touched with a dagger before taking a solemn oath of undying loyalty. Below: the oath is taken before the Worshipful Master, the chief officer of a Masonic lodge. Bottom: the candidate receives a gauge, a gavel, a chisel, and an apron—symbols of membership.

homes. As her man goes out to meet the boys for a drink or a game of poker, a baseball game or a union meeting, a woman may feel that she can practically hear the claims of family life being dropped like so many chains as he crosses the threshold. She may get the impression—and she may be right—that, out of sight of his family, he's going to behave like a carefree adolescent, rather than the grown-up man he is.

On the whole, women, even in a group, find it impossible to relapse into the carefree high spirits of their childhood. No doubt this is because women are trained to be more self-conscious than men, more aware of appearances. Possibly too, it's because a woman, once she has become a mother, never feels quite free, as a man may, to leave her responsibilities behind her. After all, a man gets used to leaving his roles as husband and father behind him when he goes off to work every morning, so that he can devote himself entirely to his role as working man during the day. A woman, on the other hand, plays the role of wife and mother 24 hours a day, and it's not so easy for her to see herself in a different light.

Be that as it may, men do seem to have this ability to feel free and enjoy a childlike sense of release in each other's company. Men, especially in groups, can forget the pressures of their world and behave like high-spirited teenagers. Such behavior, to be seen at football games and convention assemblies, seems to work as a safety valve for the tensions they feel. In fact, as women know all too well, the mischievous little boy is rarely very far beneath the skin of most men, and is only waiting for other full-grown mischievous little boys to call him out to play. It is a favorite male fantasy that despite bills, burdens, and family duties they can, whenever they wish, be irresponsible scalawags again. It is a fantasy that groups of men often act out together.

"After one of these conventions," said a policeman in a major convention town, "we've got a whole array of arrests for disturbing the peace, and they are mostly for

A friend is someone you care deeply about, someone you can trust and confide in, laugh with and
be yourself with. A friend is someone you want
to go on knowing and sharing things with as the
years go by. Not surprisingly, this description
of friendship could also be applied to a happy
marriage, and for many couples, the best friendship of all is the one they share as man and wife.

really childish pranks—a grown-up business-man, for instance, shooting people with ink from a water pistol. Not one of these guys has ever been arrested before."

Although wives often direct all kinds of accusations at their husbands about sexual orgies and whatnot at their conventions, these meetings are less marked by depravity than they are by the escapades and tom-foolery of grown men released for a while from the pressures of supporting a family, paying the mortgage, and meeting their wives' demands for everything from new appliances to sexual bliss. "We drink too much," says one conventioneer, "and we make a helluva lot of noise. And that's about the worst you can say."

Large numbers of men belong to exclusive or semi-secret organizations devoted to com-munity planning, charities, politics, or just male togetherness. Although these groups often try to support women's auxiliaries, women on the whole do not share the same need for ritualized and highly structured clubs. Even as children, it is little boys more often than little girls who organize secret clubs with special code words and meeting places. Moreover, girls are usually banned from these clubs, which, in a sense, are early expressions of the male mystique.

In adulthood, as in childhood, these highly organized, men-only clubs provide still another area for competition, achievement, and the reinforcement of manhood. "My election to a high post in our lodge," one of these club members said in a recent inter-view, "has been the high point of my life and the most satisfying thing that has ever happened to me. Nothing can compare in a man's life to being chosen for office by your brothers and peers." Though women face the fact with discomfort, some part of the need among men for these exlcusive groups is for a temporary escape from the woman's world in which demands are made upon men by women or in support of women and children.

Up to a point then, a man's friendships and get-togethers with other men seem to be vital to his well-being. Indeed, for both husband and wife, contacts and close relationships with members of their own sex are not only pleasureable, but necessary. Friendships—both separate and mutual—can satisfy needs that cannot entirely be met by the marriage partner. They can buttress marital stability, and even knit the relationship between husband and wife closer together by helping to take the burden of full emotional satisfac-tion off the marriage itself, and bring added pleasure to the individuals within it.

It sometimes happens that either the wife or the husband feels jealous of the other's friendships. This can be quite justified if either seems to be giving more of himself to his friends than to the person he married. By the same token, it can be the result of over-possessiveness, an inability to make friends of his or her own, or a sign that an insufficient effort has been made to keep the marital relationship growing.

In the long run, marriage can be the deepest friendship of all, the one with the richest potential for growth and change. Based on a bond between two people of different sexes, in many ways mysterious to one another, it can have almost endless possibilities for increased understanding, inti-macy, comfort, and love.

A Man in Love
6

"I love you." There isn't a woman alive who doesn't long to hear these words from the man she loves. Yet how often does she hear them, and when she does, can she be sure they're true? It's an age-old complaint among women that men either find it too difficult to say "I love you," or, conversely, all too easy. Certainly it can be as distressing to be told you're loved only when a persuasive masculine arm is guiding you toward the bedroom, as it is to have to ask a man for this simple reassurance of his feelings for you.

There are, of course, plenty of modern-day Don Juans who use the word "love" when "desire" is really more what they mean. "If it makes her receptive," says one such man, "I'll tell her I love her. It's faster than champagne and cheaper than a diamond ring."

Such cynicism about using the word "love" is probably far less typical of the average man than the sheer reluctance to use it at all. A snatch of dialog from a typical Hollywood movie puts it in a nutshell: "There's something you haven't told me in a long time," says the hero's wife. "What's that?" he asks. "Well, if I have to *tell* you . . ." she murmurs, looking downcast. "Oh, anyone can say 'I love you,' " he says, laughing and kissing her. "That's just corny. Besides, I'd rather show you."

In many a marriage—and indeed, in many a love affair as well—the woman waits in vain for a spontaneous declaration of love from her man. "I know he loves me," says one woman, "but if only he knew how happy it would make me to hear him say it, just once, without me prodding him."

Why should the word "love" be so much

For a woman, falling in love spells fulfillment, the long-awaited realization of her girlhood dreams. But for a man, falling in love may prove unexpectedly shattering. Less prepared for it than she, he may feel surprised and bewildered by the strength of his emotions.

easier for a woman to say—and mean—than it is for a man? Probably because the word has been a staple part of her vocabulary for a much longer time. A little girl's verbal expressions of love for her family, for example, are accepted naturally as signs of her femininity. But a small boy, at least one over the age of four or five, is usually not encouraged to go around saying; "I love my Mommy, I love my Daddy, I love my Uncle Dick." Small girls are encouraged to "love" their dolls; little boys are not encouraged to "love" dolls, or any other toys for that matter. Though little girls can show a special fondness for a particular friend, small boys are encouraged to relate to each other in a childhood version of man-to-man toughness. By the time he is ten, a boy has it firmly fixed in his mind that "love" is a sissy word, used only by girls. Within the next couple of years, that basic difference in vocabulary will have taken on a whole new dimension.

When girls reach adolescence, they become aware that there is another kind of love—romantic love—that is somehow their special province. The books and magazines they read, the soap operas and movies they see, all encourage them to dream, think, and talk about love as the peak experience awaiting them. They begin wanting to fall in love, to be loved passionately in return, to marry for love, and to live happily ever after, still madly and mutually in love with their husbands. Reality, of course, is not always so romantic. Nonetheless, most young girls devoutly hope and expect that this great and

Above: two 19th-century lovers sit by a stream on a summer's day. While he looks on shyly, she reads a sonnet that describes his love for her.
Right: a valentine, often sent with a gift, is still a cherished token of a man's affection.

beautiful thing will happen to them. The word "love" is the key to it all.

Adolescent boys on the other hand, have their minds on other things, such as making the basketball team or fixing a motorcycle. They're also busy identifying with action-type heroes whose measure of success is not how much they love or are loved by a woman, but how well they prove their skill and courage in the world of men. When they become men themselves, they are encouraged to see women less in terms of romantic fulfillment than in terms of sexual pleasure. It's all part of the male mystique. The books and magazines men read, for example, emphasize the twin masculine goals of success and sexual prowess. The whole vocabulary is oriented to action, rather than to emotion—

just as it was in their boyhood days. The word "love" is avoided as being somehow effeminate. Love, in a man's world, is a bonus, something that comes your way if you're lucky, but not your acknowledged aim in life, and certainly not something you discuss with the rest of the guys.

What you do discuss with the rest of the guys (if you're a man, that is) is sex. This is something that women find very hard to understand. How can men be so unfeeling as to wisecrack, speculate, and positively brag about sexual intimacy? Why must they see women in terms of their vital statistics and how good they might be in bed? How can they get such a kick out of looking at *Playboy* pinups or pornographic playing cards? Don't women mean anything to them as people?

Courtship in the early 18th century was an elaborate ritual. It was a woman's role to remain seemingly aloof while her suitor strove to persuade her of his passion with gestures of gallantry. In this painting, the young lady maintains an air of haughty disdain, while her wooer proffers a nosegay of flowers, no doubt accompanied by an ardent declaration of his undying devotion.

The answer to this last question is yes, emphatically so. But by and large, the only women whose finer points a man will refrain from, or refuse to, discuss are those he feels an emotional attachment to. About others, especially when he is a young men eager to prove his virility, a sort of open season prevails, as far as conversation between men is concerned.

But why? Women enjoy and think about sex too, but they don't go around casually speculating and callously joking about it all the time. The difference between men and women in this respect probably goes back to the difference in the way they are brought up. Women are encouraged to be more oriented to people and emotion right from the start. Men, on the other hand, are encouraged from childhood onward to be more oriented to objects and action. One expert has put it this way: "Men tend to 'objectify' their lives . . . while women show an opposite tendency to 'personalize'—to form a relationship, as it were, with the matter at hand. This is probably one reason why men talk about sex, about actually having sexual intercourse, without showing too much interest in who the woman is. Women, on the other hand, tend to show more interest in the person with whom they are involved."

He goes on to say that "the *idea* of sex, or the *sight* of a woman, can excite a man, while it is the *touch* of a real person that is most stimulating to a woman. The pornography, fantasies, graffiti, and sexual conversations favored by men have the form of depersonalized sexual encounters, and thus they are attractive to men but not to women . . . [But] if 'sex' were defined as sexual *relationships* rather than the isolated sexual act, women would probably prove to be more concerned with it than men."

Interesting, yes? Especially when you think about the way women are always trying to find love and sex together, while men seem capable of enjoying sex all on its own. This is particularly true of men while they are young, competing with their peers for the widest sexual experience, and, incidentally, seeking

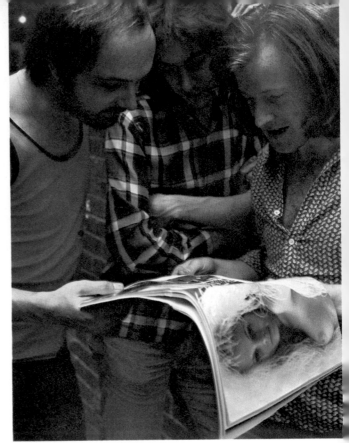

Above: a familiar scene—a group of men thoroughly enjoying themselves as they pore over the titillating contents of a girlie magazine.

Right: loving intimacy between a man and a woman brings satisfactions no mere pinup can provide.

to become knowledgeable lovers as the partner of the woman they will eventually marry.

It is while men are gaining this sexual experience—sowing their wild oats, as the expression goes—that they may occasionally take the world "love" in vain. It's easy enough to use the word as a mere ploy, but when they really mean it, when their emotions are really involved, most men find the simple phrase "I love you" amazingly hard to utter. Raised to believe that love is a woman's province, a sort of emotional equivalent to knitting, many men feel embarrassed about their true feelings. They may explain away their reluctance by calling such an admission "corny," but what they really mean is that it makes them feel awkward and a little silly. They prefer a pleasant, unquestioned and unquestioning flow of their emotions; they

prefer to *show* a woman that they care for her. Action, after all, is a man's province.

Despite their reluctance to talk about it, however, men do fall in love, and often far more wildly and romantically than women. The capacity to fall in love is one of the things that makes us human, and, where romantic passion is concerned, men are just as susceptible as any woman. What is more, they are less emotionally prepared for it when it happens. For any young woman who has read stories about love, the scenario is practically written in advance. For a young man, however, especially one who has spent his leisure time reading *True Adventure* and *Real Mechanics,* the whole thing can come as a shattering surprise.

"It would seem," says one psychotherapist, "that women are aware of love, or at least of crushes, in a highly publicized way and a lot earlier than men are. But I promise you that no grown man has ever forgotten his first love. I myself was 15 when I fell in love with a girl of 17. It was a classic case. I nearly broke my fool neck in the attempt to get her attention."

Though the good doctor probably didn't tell his friends about it at the time, he obviously suffered—and enjoyed—the pangs of love very deeply. It's quite true that falling in love—though it may come as a shock to a man—can be every bit as enthralling as it is for a woman.

What makes a man fall in love? Well, what makes a woman fall in love? For both, it usually begins with physical attraction. Then, there is usually something about the person they are attracted to that triggers off the idea that *this* could be the one—the living embodiment of all those ideal qualities they always hoped to find in a member of the opposite sex.

Wanting so much to find these desirable qualities in the person they feel drawn to, both men and women often exaggerate their beloved's potential for making them happy. Sometimes they even see this potential where it simply doesn't exist. We've all met the type of individual who always seems to fall for

People have been falling for unattainable members of the opposite sex since time began. In this 18th-century painting, a young gardener declares his hopeless passion for the lady of the house. Class distinction—and the fact that she is married already—clearly make a romantic relationship between them out of the question.

Many women seem to have a weakness for irresponsible men. This 19th-century painting depicts the plight of a woman who has married a complete ne'er-do-well. Having gambled away the family fortune (both house and furniture are up for sale), he carries on drinking champagne as though there were no tomorrow. He has even begun teaching his young son to follow in his footsteps.

impossible or unattainable people—people who are already married, for example, or who are hopelessly neurotic, weak, cruel, or alcoholic. Barring this kind of total blindness about a person, most men and women simply indulge in a bit of idealization where their beloved is concerned.

It may please a woman, for example, to see the object of her affections as combining the reckless daring of a James Bond with the dependability of a grandfather clock; the tough masculinity of an old West cowboy with the gentle wisdom of Solomon. But on the whole, women tend to be just a bit more realistic, even a bit more hardheaded, about the men they love than men are about the women they love. Most women's romantic fantasies have a practical end in view. A young couple in love may be equally blind to one another's minor shortcomings, but while the man is looking no further ahead than tomorrow or next week, the woman is probably thinking about getting married, and sizing up his potential as a husband, father, and provider.

For a man in love, the moment is now, and his particular love blindness is complicated by the confused concept of womanhood he has grown up with. In his childhood, there was the contradiction between those helpless little neighborhood girls and his competent, loving mother. Then, as he grew to manhood, there was the contradiction between the girl of his dreams—pure and innocent—and the girl of his fantasies—sexy and experienced. When he falls in love, he is likely to think he has found the perfect combination of all these contradictory feminine qualities. In her, he will find a helpless and adoring creature who is also a competent homemaker, an innocent girl next door who is also as seductive as a *Playboy* bunny, a born mother who is never too tired to be a loving wife, a model of fidelity who is also the envy of all his friends.

Women, of course, being women themselves, are quick to see just how blind a man can be when he fixes all his contradictory fantasies on a female they know well. "I remember listening to my brother-in-law,"

Left: Although it has become a joke, many a woman still dreams of being swept off her feet by a real, no-nonsense caveman type.

Right: some women only feel truly feminine when they're with an ultra-masculine male. Certainly, many women idolize this type as portrayed by the famous Hollywood he-men.

says one woman, "going on and on about this girl my husband and I introduced him to. Let me tell you what he was describing was someone as noble as Florence Nightingale with the looks of Jane Fonda. It had nothing to do with this slightly affected, desperate divorcee we knew. When he finally started talking about her marvelous eyelashes, it was all I could do to keep from telling him I had exactly the same pair in a drawer upstairs!"

Men often laugh about women's gullibility when it comes to being told they're beautiful. But men—as women know very well—are just as gullible to flattery, not only about their looks, but also about how strong and clever they are. Women learned long ago that the fastest way to a man's heart was not food, but flattery. Men pride themselves on being tougher and smarter than women. And a woman can make almost any man feel like Tarzan if she acts enough like Jane. Acting like Jane requires that she hide her own intellectual light under a bushel, and that she never display competence in fields he is supposed to be master of. It's all right for her to be a whiz at changing diapers—that's her province—but when it comes to changing tires, she'd better play dumb and helpless. That's his province.

Just how morale boosting a woman's relative weakness and dumbness can be for a man is amply demonstrated by the kind of humorous bragging sessions men go in for with each other, each one trying to prove

how much sillier, or more dependent on his superior talents his woman is than any other man's.

"Then the policeman stopped us for speeding, and Janice—she was driving—said she couldn't have been speeding because she had seen very clearly the price of a dress in a window we had just passed . . ."

"You think that's something! Listen to this one. Marianne collected six parking tickets in one afternoon."

"That's nothing. Wait till I tell you what Sally did . . ."

The other side of the coin is, of course, that women usually feel safer, more secure, with a man who has everything under control. Women usually don't mind playing down their talents if it helps their man to be stronger and more dependable. It's a two-way game. Each sex, by playing the role expected of them, encourages the other to play his or her expected role. The illusions they hold about one another help to reinforce their own identity as male and female. There's something positively bewitching about someone who can make you feel "all woman"—or, in the case of a man, "all man." As always, men and women fall in love not only with their idealized version of the other person, but also with that person's idealized version of them.

Whatever it is that's really happening when two people fall in love—whatever fantasies of themselves and the other they indulge in, whatever emotional gymnastics they put each other through—the fact remains that falling in love is one of the most exciting experiences of life for both sexes. No individual, male or female, who has experienced the joys and torments of being in love would deny this. Poets and pop song writers continue to sing its praises, and rightly. For all the sufferings, as well as the ecstasies, it brings, the capacity to fall deeply and truly in love remains one of the most delightful aspects of being alive and being human. We are, after all, the only creatures on earth who know the meaning of romantic love.

100

Romance has many moods, and for every couple in love, each step in their relationship can bring the excitement of a new discovery. Love is like a roller coaster, plunging the lover from the heights of bliss to the depths of misery—but the ride is always worth the risk.

What Makes a Man Marry

7

Gone are the days when marriage was simply taken for granted as the normal way of life for normal men and women. It's become a hot topic, endlessly analyzed and debated in books, magazines, and TV programs. What's happening to marriage? Why do marriages go wrong? What can, or should, we expect of marriage these days? How can it be made to withstand the pressures of the world we live in? As the divorce statistics go up, as more and more young people show a preference for living together without a license, as the militants among us hammer away at its disadvantages for women, marriage is being discussed and examined as never before.

Everyone has an opinion on the subject, based on his or her own experience, and bolstered by the widely differing views put forth in the media. We read, for example, that marriage is becoming an outmoded institution, badly in need of radical alterations. We read about trial marriages, and marriages entered into on the express condition that, if it doesn't work out, neither partner will object to a divorce. We even read suggestions that, with everyone living such long lives nowadays, people should plan on having a series of marriages—one for the carefree years of youth, perhaps; another for the more serious years of childbearing and child rearing; and a final one for the peaceful years of retirement when the kids have grown up and left home.

The debate goes on and on. Yet the significant factor in all this concern about marriage is the concern itself. Marriage, for all the problems it poses, continues to be something we all care about, and deeply. However difficult many individual marriages

The wedding day, with all its elaborate trappings, traditionally centers on the bride. It is usually she who wants a big wedding, and she who seems most to delight in reminiscing about it afterward. But for all the joking reluctance a bridegroom often displays about "the big day," he wouldn't be there if he didn't want to be. It takes two, after all, to make a marriage.

are, the institution itself is something we resolutely refuse to lose faith in. Despite the well-publicized figures on the poor chance of achieving continued marital bliss, men and women go right on getting married. No doubt they're aware that there may be hitches in store for them, but that certainly doesn't prevent them from getting hitched.

Below: nowadays, the wedding ceremony sets the seal on a relationship between two people who have freely chosen each other above all others.

Right: there was a time when women had no say at all about whom they married. In this painting of a Babylonian marriage market, young women are bought and sold like cattle.

Cynics might say that the reason marriage certificates continue to be issued by the millions lies in the fact that women still insist on the respectability, reassurance, and security that that little piece of paper gives them. But that would be only half the story. Most men marry because they want to, not simply to please their women, or because they have to. (Shotgun weddings are still the exception, not the rule.)

So why *do* men get married? Surely they have more to lose, in terms of pure freedom, than women do? Unmarried, they could live as they pleased, spend their money as they pleased, plan their futures as they pleased.

Why does any man voluntarily choose to tie himself to one woman and take on the whole flock of responsibilities that go with being head of a household, when the life of a swinging bachelor is supposed to be so much fun?

The reasons, of course, are many. In the first place—and most importantly—when a man falls in love with a woman, he usually wants to make her his own in some permanent way. Then too, many men (a great many more than would admit it) really want to have children. In fact, men often take a far more romantic view of their potential offspring than women do, seeing them less in such practical terms as dependents in need of food, clothing, shelter, and day-to-day care, than as miraculous products of their own creation, something to love and be proud of, to carry on the family name, to give them that final dimension of manhood, being a father.

As we all know, few men are willing to trade in their single status for that of a husband and father until they are "ready." When that happens, when a man is ripe for marriage, it usually doesn't take him long to find the right girl. So what makes a man ready to marry? Society, custom, his own background, his age, what his friends are

doing, the kind of life he's leading—all these factors play an important part in the process, just as they do for a woman.

A man is likely to start thinking about marriage sooner, for example, if his own parents were happily married. With that sort of pattern before him, he is likely to be more marriage-minded, and anxious to find a woman with whom he can enjoy the kind of happiness his parents had.

Even if his parents' marriage was not successful, and he is shy of committing himself for that reason, a man will sooner or later begin to feel a definite social pressure to marry. This pressure will increase every year the longer he stays single. Our society takes a rather dim view of the confirmed bachelor, eyeing him with suspicion rather than tolerance. "What's the matter with him?" we say, taking his stubborn singleness as a sign of some sexual or emotional abnormality. Marriage, we believe, is the human condition, and the man who continues to reject it is liable to be considered unusual, at best. Anthropologists suggest that men and women

are not monogamous by nature, but society holds a different view. The die-hard bachelor, therefore, must be prepared to bear up under the onslaughts of criticism and curiosity. The pressure to marry is every bit as great for a man as it is for a woman, and what's more, it lasts much longer. While a single woman over 40 may be given up as a hopeless case, a single man of the same age is still considered prime marriage material, not only by his family and married friends, but also by single women as young as half his age.

Oddly enough, the swinging bachelor's sexual freedom is one of the very things that can persuade him it's time to find a woman he can really love. A man with many short-term sexual relationships behind him may begin to feel that he is leading a pretty meaningless existence, without purpose or direction. He begins to want some form of premanence and continuity, some deep emotional attachment that will really mean something to him.

All around him his friends are marrying, and the contentment of the newlyweds looks

very appealing. Of course, newlyweds usually exhibit marriage at its most carefree, romantic, and companionable, and they often can't help showing off a little. Their evident satisfaction has its effect, though, and the lingering bachelor becomes convinced that this is the life for him. "I felt left out," says one man who admits that he first started thinking about marriage when all his friends got married. "I used to date a lot, but it seemed so useless compared with the lives my friends were leading."

To the bachelor's envy of his· friends'

Above: why does a man marry? One of the old-est reasons is simply that he gets tired of bachelorhood. Even the carefree dandies of the early 19th century —shown here cavorting with equally sprightly young ladies—wound up preferring the settled comforts of marriage.

Right: having an end-less supply of pretty girls at his beck and call may sound like a man's idea of heaven. But, as many a bachelor has discovered, wining and dining them, and constantly having to be on the make, can be exhausting and ulti-mately unsatisfying.

Perhaps the most compelling reason behind a man's decision to marry is the desire to create his own family. With a loving wife and children, a man can feel that his life has real meaning.

contentment may be added a growing disenchantment with the life he's leading—or supposed to be leading. It may not sound very romantic, but it is a fact that many men begin to think of marriage not only because they feel lonely and in need of love and companionship, but also because they find bachelorhood just too demanding. Sexual freedom can be very hard work.

"You're constantly in a state of courtship," one ex-bachelor said of his so-called swinging life. "You're always on your best behavior. It all sounds glamourous—after all, as a bachelor you've got plenty of money to spend on restaurants, cars, young girls. The trouble is you can never really relax, you can never just be yourself. I know this sounds silly, but you're expected to make love, or try to, even if you don't really feel like it. After a while, you really long to be with just one woman, you want to have supper at home, put your feet up. It's the constant performance that gets you down."

Men's magazines, which seem to advocate a life of eternal bachelordom, sell, in fact, to a very young readership (in terms of maturity, if not always in years), a male readership that sees only the joys of sexual freedom, without any of its stresses and hardships. A man well into his 30's, for example, dating an 18-year-old girl, may enjoy the illusion of being as young as she is, but ultimately finds himself tired out, even bored, by her very youth. Moreover, the competition for attractive girls is fierce among single men, and keeping pace with every other unmarried Tom, Dick, and Harry can make it difficult to keep up with an increasing work load, especially as a man gets older.

There is a further pressure put on single men to marry, and that is to prove their maturity. Our society regards any normal red-blooded male who chooses to live solely for himself as something of a selfish loner. Taught to be competitive in all areas of his life, a man can succumb to the idea of marriage as another way to prove that he is as good or better than any other male. Big companies encourage this competition by making marriage almost an unwritten requirement for promotion, thus suggesting that the man unwilling to assume responsibility in his private life will be unable to assume it in his working life. Theoretically, marriage steadies a man, and statistically, an overwhelming number of successful executives are, in fact, married. Moreover, when an ambitious young man gets around to thinking about marriage, he may very well keep his eye open for a woman who will enhance his image and contribute to his success.

So you see, there's a lot more to being ready for marriage—at least where a man is concerned—than meets the eye. Probably few men are aware of all the influences acting upon them when they begin to think about getting married, but they're present all the same. When a man is ripe for marriage, it won't take him long to find a woman equally ready to marry. Will she really turn out to be the right one for him? Will he turn out to be the right one for her? Ah, that's another story. Falling in love is easy. So is getting married. But marriage itself can prove the most demanding—as well as the most rewarding—experience either will ever have.

The Married Man
8

Whatever it is that makes a man choose a particular woman to be his wife, and whatever it is that makes her want to say "yes" to him, one thing is sure: they are not going to live happily ever after. Unlike fairy tales and soap operas, the story does not end with the hero and heroine going off into the sunset together. Life can be just as dramatic as literature—sometimes a lot more so—but it certainly doesn't have such neat endings. The curtain doesn't come down on the happy pair that has at long last joined two lives in holy wedlock. On the contrary, it's just going up. Before the twosome lies a great adventure, full of as many joys and sorrows as any fictional romance—and twice as real, especially for the heroine.

"Remember that a businessman's wife can count for a lot in his professional life," states a handbook especially written for trainee executives' wives. "It is her job to maintain a living standard that is not too lavish for her husband's income. She must also be prepared to entertain, no matter how simply, on short notice. When her husband is a struggling trainee, with so many new concepts to absorb, she must be patient and understanding. Later she will share in his achievements and a lot of what he accomplishes will be thanks to her. An understanding, charming wife who is well-groomed and gets along with others can be a business executive's greatest asset."

The thoroughly married man. Stalled amidst the groceries while he waits for his wife to collect those last items on her list, he leans heavily on the cart, and smiles a wry smile. "So this is marriage," he might be thinking. "Ten years ago, I'd never have believed I'd be standing here."

It sounds like a tall order. It is a tall order. But it's surprising how many men take it as a matter of course that their wives will not only meet all these requirements, but will also be an exciting sexual partner, a loving and efficient mother, a talented cook, and an expert housekeeper. What's even more surprising is the number of women who manage to be all or most of these things, all or most of the time.

We have all heard it said that far too much is expected of women today, and that they are wearing themselves out trying to play too many different roles. There is no doubt a great deal of truth in this, but there are, in fact, many women who revel in their ability to play these different roles and play them well. When it comes to a real consensus, more women would probably reach agreement on the subject of the roles their husbands play, or fail to play, in marriage.

How often have you heard women complain that their husbands don't understand them, don't help them enough, or let them down by being inconsiderate, uncooperative, or uncommunicative? How often have you complained about these things yourself? If you've never had cause to, you're a lucky woman, married to a very rare man. Though generalizations are always dangerous, it might be said that where marriage is concerned, men tend to expect more of their wives than they do of themselves.

Why should this be? If there is any answer at all, it lies in the fact that men are truly the more romantic of the two sexes. At heart, however intuitive and illogical women are said to be, they tend to be more practical and realistic about human relationships than

Every married couple has its own way of parceling out responsibilities. Who makes most of the decisions in your household? For the answer, take a look at our chart. You may be surprised to see just how many decisions you make separately and how many you and your husband make together.

Who proposed?

Who decided where the wedding was?

Who decided on the honeymoon

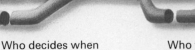

Who makes the financial decisions?

In whose name is the checking account?

Who writes out checks for bills?

Who decides when to make love?

Who takes responsibility for contraception?

Who decides wh to have children

Who sends family birthday cards?

With whose relatives is the most time spent?

Who chooses th children's names

Whose premarriage friends are seen frequently?

Who decides how each should vote?

Who decides on vacations?

Who chooses furniture?

Who chooses china?

Who does the housework?

Your Marriage Partnership: Who Decides What?

Whose name is it in ?

Who decides whether
wife should work ?

Who decides if
incomes should be shared ?

Who decides which
house to buy ?

Who decides when
to move ?

Who gets up when
they cry at night ?

Who takes care
of the babies ?

Who disciplines
the children ?

Who helps with
homework ?

Who takes responsibility
for family's health ?

Who arranges vacations ?

Who decides when
to go out ?

Who decides where
to go ?

Decisions taken by.

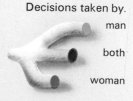

man

both

woman

Who deals with
repairmen ?

Whose food tastes
are catered to ?

Who plans the meals ?

When men marry, they are really leaving a club, the carefree society of bachelors anonymous. But when women marry, they enter a club, the sisterhood of wives. Belonging to this sisterhood can bring a sense of fulfillment, of sharing a special world that excludes the non-marrieds.

the male of the species. This may explain why men often find it more difficult than women to recognize and meet the complex needs of the person they marry.

Of course, both wife and husband are bound to be slightly disappointed when it comes to reconciling their romantic ideal with the reality of marriage. But, of the two, it's often the man who finds the adjustment a little more difficult. One expert on the subject put it this way: "Men are raised to expect the woman they love, and the one who loves them, to become a sort of extension of themselves, loving, understanding, tender, always agreeable. Woman are raised to believe that basically all men are tough outside, with the hearts of little boys. Frankly, women are closer to the truth. It is the men who are more often disappointed and confused when they discover that the lovely symbol of perfect womanhood, their romance, is a real human being when they marry her. I even know of one man who was absolutely distraught when he learned that his wife was better at keeping the accounts than he; he thought it was unnatural, a threat to his manhood!"

Possibly a woman finds it easier to adjust to the habits and idiosyncracies, the peculiar strengths and weaknesses, of the person she marries, because all her life she has been encouraged to be flexible and aware of the needs of others. She's been brought up to be concerned with emotions and relationships, and perhaps for this reason, she's better prepared to make adjustments. A man, for whom this kind of close and complex relationship is a relatively new kind of challenge, may be surprised at just how much

is going to be expected of him in the way of tolerance, cooperation, understanding, and flexibility.

In marrying, many women feel that they have achieved their primary goal, realized their major ambition. Many men, on the other hand, see marriage as a kind of bonus, a logical step in their destiny to be sure, but not their chief aim in life. For a woman, getting married can bring the same sense of accomplishment a pilot feels when he gets his wings after so many hours of flying solo. Marriage puts her on an equal footing with other women who have accomplished the same thing. For a man, however, it may seem like a sort of fringe benefit, something

that will provide him with an endless supply of pleasure and comfort. If anything, he sees himself as retaining a certain distinction, as not really being like the other married men he knows.

This romantic notion of himself applies to his beloved as well. After marriage, most men expect their wives to remain the same attentive, attractive, even-tempered people they fell in love with. Women, on the other hand, take it for granted that after marriage, everything in their lives will change—including the men they married. It comes as an unwelcome surprise to many young wives when their husbands don't change in certain respects, and go on acting like young bachelors. But it comes as an even more unwelcome surprise to many young husbands when their wives do change, and, seemingly overnight, start-acting like stolid middle-aged matrons.

"We used to have a lot to talk about," said one puzzled male newlywed, "and I thought she was interested in a lot of the things that interested me. But soon after the honeymoon, she began behaving just like my mother used to, complaining about what time I came in, that kind of thing. We had our first fight one Sunday when I wanted to relax and she wanted me to put up the screens. It wasn't putting up the screens that bothered me, it was the way she asked me, nagging, like I owed it to her, just like Mom used to talk to my Dad."

No doubt, if there were more premarital honesty, there would be less postmarital disappointment on both sides. Even those who have moral and religious scruples against sexual experimentation before marriage are all for young people getting to know each other as well as possible before marriage. But society puts such pressure on its young people to marry—and to marry for love—that they are often unwilling to present a true and honest picture of themselves lest they fail to capture the object of their affections. Alas, this is even more true of women than it is of men. It is hardly surprising, therefore, that men, encouraged by women themselves to believe in the possibility of feminine perfection, are often taken aback by the real complexities and contradictions of the women they marry.

Although the first flush of marriage may make him forget it temporarily, the average man remembers at some point in his married life the romantic ideal he once thought he'd found. It is then that he may look at his wife, by now occupied 25 hours a day looking after the house and kids, and see that he did not, after all, marry the happy blonde always ready for a laugh, or the shy brunette with a smoldering soul, or any of the other female stereotypes that might have been his dream girl once. He sees, in fact, that he is married to another complete, sometimes difficult, and sometimes inscrutable, human being, who may even be starting to get plump and resemble her mother. It is at this point in their married lives that men show a marvelous blindness to their own spreading waistlines, stubborn streaks, and sundry other faults and follies. It is at this point that many men begin to feel harried by their responsibilities, let down by their wives, and disappointed by the way things have turned out generally. It is often at this point that the man who married so eagerly for serenity, comfort, and companionship may begin to look at the bachelors he knows with some envy.

"Whenever I see a friend getting married," said one married man at a pre-wedding stag party, "I really want to stop him. I don't mean for good or anything, but just to make him stop and think about what he's doing, about the payments on the washing machine, about a house full of diapers, about how his wife is going to change as soon as she gets that band of gold around her finger. Oh boy, the things I could tell him! But he wouldn't listen. He's only thinking about the little doll he's marrying, and the honeymoon."

Although we all believe that men are polygamous by nature, as though polygamy were some odd male complaint, there is a good chance that few men would ever think in terms of more than one woman if that one woman was really the person they thought she was when they married her. But aren't they asking too much of her? Yes, indeed; but remember, they've usually been encouraged to believe that they've found everything they always wanted in that one feminine creature.

Every marriage reaches a critical point. In some marriages that point can be the beginning of a renewed, deeper, and steadier affection. In others, it can be the beginning of the proverbial seven-year-itch, with all the betrayals, big or little, that that can entail.

Whether or not the double standard of sexual behavior is a valid fact hardly matters as long as people think that it is. Men as a

Right: a tongue-in-cheek cartoon of a couple before and after marriage. Turn it upside down, and you will see what the cartoonist means.

AFTER MARRIAGE

BEFORE MARRIAGE

Below: "Faults on both sides". This 19th-century painting illustrates one of those sad moments in marriage, when neither of the partners knows how to bridge the gulf that has arisen between them.

rule believe in the double standard (it is to their advantage, after all) and live by it, or like to think they could. With a background of emotional fulfillment at home—knowing they are loved and needed by their wives and children—many men excuse their occasional infidelities as "just one of those things," or "nothing important," or "just a one-night-stand." Few of them realize, where these minor peccadillos are concerned, just how great a risk they are taking. For, in any intimate encounter between a man and a woman, there is always the possibility of an emotional, as well as physical, betrayal of the woman he loves and is married to. In most cases, a man manages to get away with it, to have his fun without any emotional involvement. Probably this is because men, far more than women, are able to objectify and compartmentalize sexual relations.

There are many marriages in which the wife has found out about her husband's occasional falls from grace, and has forgiven him. There are very few marriages in which the husband has found out about his wife's infidelity and forgiven *her*. "Whatever the causes and whatever you might think of it," one marriage counselor has said, "sex is still a more complicated act for a woman than it is for a man, and it still involves a lot more than her body. Therefore a husband whose wife has been unfaithful knows that she has given to some other man more than just her physical presence. She has given something which her husband feels he has every right to call his own."

The counselor, himself a man, went on to say: "There is still in marriage an element of possessiveness. The wife still does seem to belong to her husband. When a wife is unfaithful and the husband finds out about it, the news is often taken as an absolutely shattering betrayal and much less forgivable than a man's infidelity is to most well-balanced women."

Certainly, a surprising number of men admit that one of the reasons they married in the first place was to prevent the woman they desired from desiring others or being desired by them. Obviously a married woman does not suddenly become unattractive to all men save her husband. But the marriage contract—and the fact that she is out of harm's way at home most of the time—do seem to put up a fairly effective barrier between her and extramarital affairs.

Why are men unfaithful? Is it only because they're out in the world and confronted with

more temptations than their wives? This is one reason, of course, but there are others. One of these is their essential romanticism, their continuing belief that somewhere they will find that perfect image of womanhood, adoring, uncomplicated, undemanding, granting pleasure without ever inflicting pain.

There is another reason, however, and often-times a far more potent one, and that is that they feel neglected by their wives. Most men like to be pampered. They want maternal tenderness, maternal attentiveness, and maternal devotion—all provided by a woman they desire. Ideally, that woman is their wife, and most women respond well to their husbands' need for mothering, at least in the early days of their marriage. Then, of course, they begin to have children,

Above: physical intimacy with another woman carries with it the risk of an emotional involvment. Most men realize this, and shy away from any really serious relation-ships outside marriage.

Right: traditionally, a wife's infidelity has always been viewed with special disapproval. This moralistic 19th-century painting shows the dire consequences of a wife's adultery. There has been a fight between her lover and her husband. As the lover escapes, the wife begs for her dying hus-band's forgiveness.

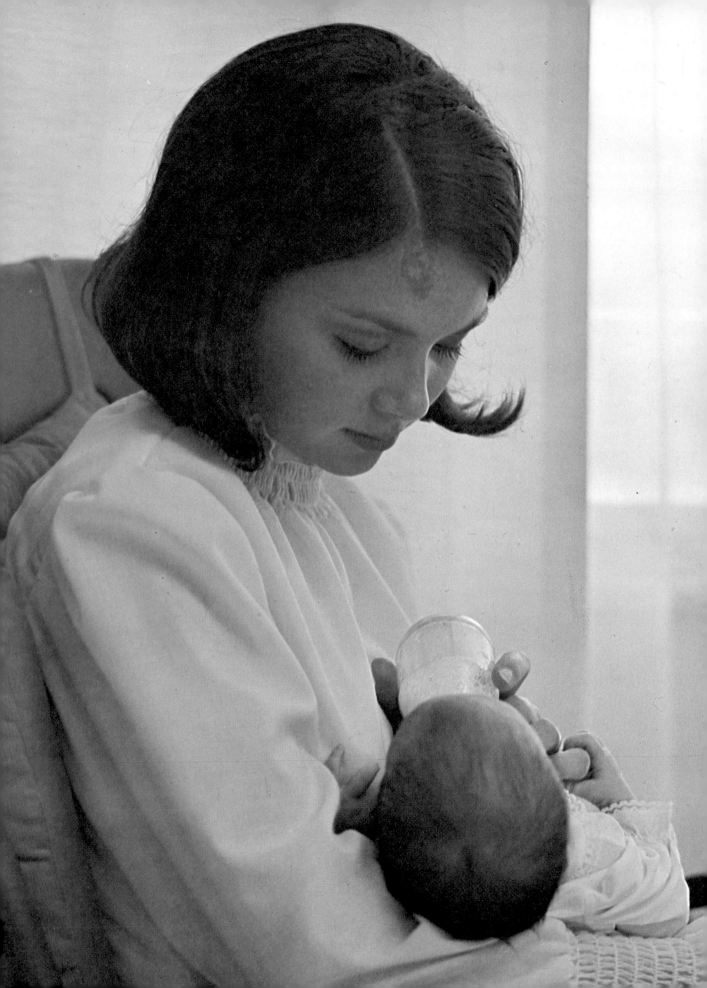

and they switch their mothering instincts to them. It's all perfectly natural, but they may fail to realize that their husbands are bound to suffer withdrawal symptoms when they are suddenly deprived of their wives' concentrated attentions, and are expected overnight to become undemanding, responsible, serious providers.

Nothing on earth changes the basic marital relationship more than eight pounds or so of a new human being. As much as he loves and is proud of the child, the husband now has a competitor in his own home. His peace is shattered, and his wife, who may at this time be tired and moody, does not seem to love him any more. Many women become so totally absorbed with their child, or children, that they do neglect their husbands. A man may begin to feel a little bit like the mate of a black widow spider; he's done his duty, fathered the offspring, and now would he please disappear. All the sympathy of friends and family goes to the busy young mother. No one bothers to consider the plight of the poor young husband, who is really not unlike the first-born child in a family, ousted by a younger rival. Yet again, the woman he married is not the woman he's living with.

In a society in which the husband's chief job is to support his wife and their children, he is out working during most of his children's waking hours, and sees them only rarely. In such a society it is understandable that the paternal urge has been allowed to languish, while the maternal urge has grown all-powerful in the home. People have not always been like this, with their labors so utterly divided by gender. The prehistoric hunter, for example, went out after game only when his family was hungry. The rest of the time he worked at home with his wife sorting grain and nuts, and probably caring for the children. When men became farmers,

they had the long winter months to share with their families, and when summer came, they needed their families to work with them. Nowadays, however, the division between home life and work life is so sharp that, while many women complain about being relegated to the kitchen and the supermarket, men could justifiably complain that they see hardly anything of the children for whose nourishment and welfare they are responsible, and for whom they work.

Men do care about their children, because they *are* their children; and men are perfectly capable of sharing equally in children's upbringing, provided their wives encourage them to participate right from the beginning, and don't make them feel like an outsider—a mere dull provider who knows nothing about what goes on at home. It is not only to a wife's advantage, but also very much to her children's, and still more to her husband's, to include her husband as much as possible in the raising of their children, and to involve him with more than mere bills and complaints when he comes home at night.

"Frankly, I was useless around the house," says one man in the throes of a divorce. I was always either making so much noise I'd wake the baby, or I would come home to dead silence, my supper in the oven, my wife too sleepy to wait up for me. All I did was pay bills. I guess I loved my kids, but I never saw them, I never really knew them. Some days I felt really resentful, shut out, nothing but a meal ticket. It was on one of those days that I went out on this terrific toot. Then I started playing around with other women. Well, at least they paid some attention to me."

Perhaps this man is just a little boy at heart, who needs his wife's attention as he used to need his mother's. But that is what he bargained for when he got married, and she must have known it. Someone who can devote herself to her children, like the woman under discussion, should certainly be able to comfort another one, even if he is her husband.

Today, the demands and pressures of man's life have an insidious way of driving a wedge between him and his children. A wife can do much to help her husband realize his potential as a father by making sure that he has ample opportunities to enjoy the company of their sons and daughters.

Perhaps, too, the man we quoted is more to blame for this unhappy situation than he realizes. If he never came home till late at night, it's hardly any wonder that he rarely saw his children, found his supper in the oven, and his wife asleep in bed. Again, marriage is a two-way street.

Although there are men whose continual absence from home in the evening is directly responsible for the alienation and sense of isolation they feel, there are probably many more whose wives do tend, unconsciously, to shut them out of the family. Children, and the emotional fulfillment that comes from living as a family—with all its tensions, as well as its pleasures—can mean far more to a man than most women realize. Most men, too, tend to be unaware of its possibilities. But any man who has not only seen, but also helped, his children grow up, knows that

he—and his children—are the richer for it.

Studies of divorced men support this view in a sadly back-handed sort of way. The majority of divorced men remarry within three years. Why? Chiefly because, although they may not have enjoyed the stresses of family life, they miss it terribly. "I just couldn't get used to no kids around the house and nobody to fight with," says one man who remarried after a couple of years of renewed freedom. Indeed, it's an unhappy fact that many men discover only after a divorce how very much their children meant to them. A good deal of heartache lies behind those weekly visits by the ex-husband and father. The law requires that he go on supporting his little brood, but in a very real sense, he has lost them forever.

Probably fewer marriages would end in divorce if both partners expected, not less of each other, but more of themselves. More than one expert on the subject has stated that before anything else, both husband and wife should have a clear picture of who they themselves really are—their own particular strengths and weaknesses, needs and habits,

What is a wife? Ideally, an exciting sexual partner, an expert cook and housekeeper, a charming hostess, a patient mother, and, above all, a loving and devoted companion. What is a husband? Ideally, a man who appreciates every talent she possesses and forgives those she doesn't.

abilities and limitations. With this in mind, they should then try to recognize and understand the various facets of the person they are married to. But above all, they must reach out to that person and give as much as they can of themselves to him or her.

This all sounds like very hard work, especially when both partners usually have so many other pressing things on their minds. But if a marriage is to grow, to take the hurdles it will inevitably face, the two people within it must be willing to put something more than their mere presence into it. Both husband and wife will change over the years, not only because their personalities are still developing, but also because marriage itself,

living so closely with another person, gradually shapes and alters them. Whether or not they change together, along parallel lines, depends to a large degree on whether or not they are willing to face the differences and conflicts between them, and work them out. Those who are unwilling to do so, who simply shrug their shoulders and refuse to talk about it, or give up trying to understand what makes the other person feel and act as they do, are taking a chance on letting their relationship stagnate and disintegrate. It's not always the best policy to avoid quarrels. Silent defeatism can, in some cases, have much more serious consequences than noisy disagreement. "I'd rather fight than switch," may be the best approach when it comes to something really important in the marriage.

The sociologist Vance Packard, after a four-year study of American marriages, concluded that the following ingredients were the keynote to most successful marriages:

1. A large capacity for affection through thoughtfulness.
2. Emotional maturity.
3. The ability to communicate effectively and appealingly.
4. A zest for mutual enjoyment.
5. The ability to handle tensions and differences constructively.
6. A playful approach to sex.
7. Knowledge and acceptance of each other's limitations.

It is notable that Packard's list consists entirely of intangibles; there isn't a single reference to looks, living standards, or earning capacity in the whole bunch. Even more interesting is the fact that love and consideration come at the top of the list, while "a playful approach to sex" comes near the bottom. This is curious, because, as various surveys show, young, unmarried men tend to put these desirable qualities in reverse order. Many bachelors' first priority

125

in an ideal wife is "sexiness," with "affectionateness and considerateness" coming way down the list (after such things as "good housekeeper," "good cook," "good mother," "good hostess"). So why the reversal after marriage? Does a happy sex life become less important to a happy marriage as the years go by?

Not at all. Remember, a "playful approach to sex" *is* one of the seven ingredients Packard found essential to most happy marriages. But it is only one of seven. While a successful sexual relationship lies at the heart of a good marriage and sheds its glow on all the other aspects of sharing a life together, it won't serve to cement the relationship if everything else is missing. On the contrary, the best marital sex lives have been known to crumble in an atmosphere of mutual distrust, intolerance, and lack of concern. By the same token, a couple's sexual happiness is likely to flourish in a context of mutual honesty, consideration, and generosity.

Any difficulty in marriage—be it sexual, emotional, social, or financial, can, of course, be exaggerated out of all proportion. In many ways, a woman's role in dealing with marital problems is the harder because she has less opportunity to get away from it all by plunging herself into an entirely different set of challenges. Not being surrounded by other adults all day, as her husband is at his place of work, she has more opportunity to dwell on her problems and wonder how she'll ever solve them. Perhaps this is one reason why so many women are up in arms today. They have plenty to do—often too much to do— but most of it is directly connected with their life as wives and mothers.

Yet women do have an advantage, in that they are generally more attuned to their own emotions and those of others than their equally harassed husbands. And their capacity to understand themselves and the men they are married to can make a great deal of difference in the life they share together, and the kind of relationship that develops between them. For a marriage, a good marriage, is a growing thing. And possibly the most important moment in its growth is the point at which both partners cease being romantically in love, and begin truly to love.

One expert on marriage has put it this way: "However differently they express it, both men and women are looking in marriage for the satisfaction of a basic human need: that of being loved and needed by another, and of feeling that they are important to one other human being. Whatever their failures, however humdrum their existence, their significance is assured if they are of emotional importance to another. Men, no less than women, seek to satisfy this basic need when they marry."

So fundamental a statement about human nature cannot be denied. But every other generalization—where both men and women are concerned—is open to debate. There is no real answer to the question, "What makes men tick?", because every individual man is different from every other. We can laugh and wonder, complain and speculate about the male of the species, but a full understanding of what goes on in any man's mind and heart will always be just beyond our reach. As every woman knows, it can take a lifetime to learn just a little bit about the man she loves.

Questions & Answers

Each of us has a story. In fact, each of us *is* a story, with as many conflicts, crises, and crucial episodes as any good novel. Perhaps the chief protagonist in every woman's life story is the man she loves and marries. Certainly, getting married itself will be a major turning point in her life. What happens then? From that moment on, her life ceases to be entirely her own, and becomes fused with that of a person she is only just beginning to know, and who is only just beginning to know her. From that moment on, both partners have committed themselves to a relationship that may challenge their individual capacities in a thousand different ways. How resourcefully they meet those challenges will have far-reaching effects on them as individuals, as well as on the life they share. For there are always three identities in every marriage: the wife and her husband as separate entities, and the two of them together, growing and functioning as a unit. The ultimate strength of their marriage will be rooted in the developing strength of this third, marital identity.

Every marriage presents its own unique combination of challenges for the man and woman involved, but certain marital problems are, by their very nature, more likely to arise than others. In these cases, mere statistics on how many married couples have faced them are less helpful than examples of how couples have surmounted them. For this reason, we have selected a few of the most widespread marital problems and, by means of questions, answers, and case histories, illustrate ways in which some married couples have tackled them.

Of course, there can be no sure-fire recipe for success in marriage. But, where any marital difficulty is concerned—be it emotional, sexual, social, or financial—it is often possible to benefit from the experience of others. A little insight into the way "the other half" thinks, and a new approach to shared problems, can mean the difference between frustrating deadlock and satisfying wedlock.

In her roles as daughter, wife, and mother, a woman's capacity for understanding the men in her life is constantly put to the test. As many a woman has discovered, building a good relationship with the men she loves depends a great deal on her capacity to understand herself.

129

Interpersonal Problems

I can't remember the last time he and I had a real conversation together, and I don't mean about which TV program to watch or whether the car needs an overhaul. I mean about things that really matter. I try to get through to him sometimes, but it's like talking to a brick wall. What makes him shut himself off from me this way?

Betsy, married for six years, felt misunderstood and neglected by her husband Ted, because he never seemed to want to talk when he came home. After a full day of looking after their two small children, she desperately wanted adult conversation, and when Ted turned a deaf ear, she became angry and resentful. One day, she blew up at him and told him she was going out of her mind with loneliness and boredom. If he didn't talk to her, she didn't know what she was going to do. "Well, what do you want me to talk about?" he said. "All you do at night is complain about what a hard day you've had. It makes me feel guilty, and I don't dare say anything about myself. You don't act as though you'd want to hear it anyway."

This came as a blow to Betsy—but when she thought about it, she realized that she did, in fact, tend to complain a lot to Ted, and rarely asked him about his job and what kind of day he'd had. From then on, she stopped greeting him at the door with her woes and worries, and began encouraging him to tell her more about his own day. By being more eager to listen than to be listened to, she succeeded in reopening the lines of communication, an achievement that gave them a new sense of closeness.

Every man finds it easier to talk when he knows he has a sympathetic audience. But it sometimes happens that, however ready to listen a wife may be, she still cannot get her husband to talk to her. This can be especially troubling when he becomes unusually quiet, and she knows that something is worrying him. In such cases, the direct approach rarely works. Questions such as "What's the matter?" "Why won't you tell me?" "Is it something I've done?" "Is it your job?" "Don't you feel well?" are likely to drive him still further into his shell, even if she has hit upon what's wrong. It's a proven fact that men tend to be less verbal about their anxieties than women, especially if these anxieties concern their masculine role as provider and head of household. Many men, however, would welcome the chance to discuss their problems with their wives, provided they aren't expected to come out with it all at once. Here, a wife can help her husband by taking an indirect approach—by drawing him into conversation about everyday matters, asking his advice, and showing that she values it. The important thing is that she convey her respect for him and her readiness to share problems with him. In this way, she can do much to encourage him to confide in her.

Finally, there are some men who are by nature rather quiet and reserved. Such men often find it difficult to discuss things with anyone, even their wives. Usually, a woman is aware of this trait in the man she loves before she marries him—though this may not stop her from thinking that marriage will change him. Just as often, he himself has unconsciously misled her by being more talkative before they married than afterward. This apparent change in him need not be taken as a sign that he has become bored or disinterested in her. On the contrary, it is often proof of how relaxed and comfortable he feels in her presence. As one such quiet man finally explained to his wife when she expressed concern about his uncommunicativeness, "Honey, it does me good just to be with you. One of the things I've always loved about you is that you seem to understand me without a whole lot of talk."

Indeed, the ability to share amiable silences is often a sign of true harmony between a husband and wife. Nor should it be forgotten that non-talkers are not necessarily uncommunicative. With those they love, they often rely on a private language of smiles and frowns, hugs and simple phrases to convey what others might need many words to say. Understanding this kind of personal shorthand is part and parcel of loving and living with a man who is "strong but silent."

My husband is absolutely helpless when it comes to looking after himself. He leaves it to me to lay out his clothes in the morning and pick them up wherever he's dropped them at night. He never cleans out the tub, never knows where he's put things, can't even make himself a sandwich when he's hungry. I suppose it's because his mother did everything for him when he was a boy, but for heaven's sake, I'm not his mother. Is there anything I can do to change him?

This woman is probably right in guessing that her husband never learned to do things for himself because his mother always did them for him. This makes it pretty difficult to change his habits because he obviously sees it as a woman's job to look after his creature comforts. No amount of nagging, as his wife has probably discovered, will bring about a change in his ways. She could try a more dramatic approach, by simply refusing to pick up after him, find things for him, and so forth. But she would have to remain steadfast in her resolve, no matter how bewildered and annoyed he might feel about her change in attitude—and no matter how messy the house might become as a result. What any wife should ask herself before taking this kind of stand is, "Is it worth it?" However irritated she may get at times about his habitual reliance on her, it's just possible that in her heart of hearts she takes a secret delight in it as proof of her indispensability to the man she loves.

We're always fighting. The least little thing sets us off, and then we just go on and on at each other. My girlfriend says she'd rather fight than endure the kind of silent treatment she gets from her husband. But I don't know. My quarrels with my husband never seem to solve anything. They just leave me feeling depressed. How can I put an end to this constant bickering?

A certain amount of tension is inevitable in every marital relationship. Indeed, a marriage without it is a marriage without vitality. Where never a cross word is uttered, the husband and wife may either have stopped caring about each other, or be too frightened of their real feelings to voice them. Whatever else we promise when we make our wedding vows, we do not—cannot—promise never to disagree, feel angry, or lose our temper. When two people share as much together as they do in marriage, they are bound to come into conflict occasionally. The important thing is not the conflict, but how it's handled.

Some couples have learned the happy

knack of agreeing to disagree about certain things. Others have reached a sort of tacit understanding that allows each of them to win some of the time, but neither all of the time. In still other marriages the more dominant partner always wins, while the more submissive one just gives in—and not always gracefully. Perhaps the most painful situation is that in which one partner simply turns off when the other gets angry, and goes into a sulky silence that can last for hours, days, or even weeks. This can be unbearable for the other person, not only because he or she is denied resolution to the quarrel, but because he must endure the silent treatment until his partner decides to stop punishing him.

By far, the majority of married couples, however, resort to outright quarreling to settle their differences. Some quarrels clear the air and result in a feeling of relief and mutual understanding. With the issue settled, and the tensions released, making up can be all the sweeter. Some quarrels, on the other hand, leave neither partner feeling satisfied. This is especially true when the quarrel is one they've had numerous times before, or when it seems that one argument just leads to another. In cases like this, a sort of chain reaction is set up. Still depressed and irritated by the last unresolved argument, neither partner is in a frame of mind to deal rationally with the next disagreement.

When a situation reaches this point, it may be best for the couple to get away from each other for a short time, in order to let their emotions cool down. It may then be possible for them to take a good hard look at what they're actually fighting about. It may be that both are simply overworked and overtired, and are unwittingly expressing their frustrations by finding fault with each other. Trivial annoyances can, in such cases, seem to be reasonable bones of contention. Sometimes merely explaining why they feel so tense—and making it clear that the other is in no way to blame for the mood they're in—puts things into perspective.

Another constructive approach to quarreling is to limit the argument to the issue at stake. When a person gets riled, it is all too easy to throw in every grievance they can think of, from "You're never home in time for dinner," to "You always spend too much money," to "You don't understand what I have to put up with all day," to "I don't know why I ever married you in the first place." (It's a good idea, by the way, to refrain from using those two infuriating starters—"You *never* . . . " and "You *always* . . . ") By sticking to the main point, both parties can avoid the pain of saying the kind of things that are hard to forget afterward.

By the same token, a couple might find that the trivial matters that initiate their quarrels are really only the tip of the iceberg. There may be some deeper reason for their conflicts—some basic dissatisfaction or anxiety that they have not as yet been able to acknowledge, even to themselves. If, on looking closely at their true feelings about themselves and their marriage, they discover that there is something they have been afraid to talk about, they must find the courage to bring it out into the open. One serious conversation, with honesty on both sides, can do much to defuse a highly charged situation. It can also create a channel of real communication that will make future disagreements less threatening.

Arguing need not drive a couple apart. It is only natural for a husband and wife to find themselves at odds from time to time. But if their disagreements are to be a positive, rather than a destructive, force in their relationship, they must learn the art of quarreling constructively.

I can't laugh at mother-in-law jokes because my husband's mother is a real problem. She just can't seem to accept the fact that her son has grown up and has a life of his own. We pay her regular visits, but this doesn't satisfy her. She's always calling up to talk to "her boy," and usually finds some reason

why he should drop everything and go over there to help her with something. He resents this, but not half as much as I do. What can I do about it?

Barbara had exactly this kind of problem. Her mother-in-law was a widow with a minor heart ailment. Though her doctors assured her she would probably live to be a hundred, she was constantly worried about her health, and, in fact, used her weak heart as an excuse to keep her only son Jim at her beck and call. Even during his and Barbara's honeymoon, she insisted that they leave the number at which they could be reached in case she had an attack.

Her demands seemed to increase tenfold after they had settled into their new home. She called Jim daily to describe her aches and pains, and frequently broke down and cried if he couldn't find the time to take her to the doctor's or stop off on his way home with a prescription. Though Jim knew she was being unreasonable, he found it hard to say "no" to her. He could never be sure until he saw her that she was really all right.

Barbara put up with it at first, but soon came to resent these continual maternal demands on her husband very deeply. She began to think that Jim's mother was trying to take him away from her. It was clear, in any case, that her mother-in-law's ultimate aim was to get Jim so worried that he'd ask her to come and live with them. Faced with this possibility, Barbara decided to step in. Always before, she had let Jim handle the situation, but now she made up her mind to try a new tactic. If it was sympathy, concern, and attention his mother wanted, she would supply it herself. She began phoning her mother-in-law daily, sometimes twice-daily, to ask how she was, and listened patiently to the inevitable list of complaints. Explaining that she herself was seeing less of Jim because he had so much work to do, she told her mother-in-law that she was willing and able to come over any time she needed help with anything.

Delighted at this new concern for her welfare—and from such an unexpected source at that—Barbara's mother-in-law responded eagerly. Jim's sympathy was something she had always had to work for. Barbara's, on the other hand, was offered freely and willingly. Before long, the would-be invalid had switched her dependence from her son to her sympathetic daughter-in-law.

Of course, assuming this burden was not altogether easy for Barbara. It was tedious and time consuming taking Jim's place as the ever-ready listener and errand runner. But it was an exchange she was prepared to make. It took the pressure off her husband, and neutralized his mother's hold over him. Moreover, because it was something Barbara herself had chosen to do, it was also something she could handle and keep in perspective. Perhaps the greatest benefit of all was Jim's obvious admiration and gratitude for her solution to their problem.

Before I married my husband, I had no idea what a drag his interest in sports would turn out to be. Winter, summer, spring, and fall, he spends half his time either going to games or watching them on TV. I couldn't care less about sports, and I think it's selfish of him to keep on with this hobby of his when he knows I can't share it. Am I being unfair?

There's no easy answer to this question, simply because, as many a wife has discovered, separating her man from his favorite hobby can create more problems than it solves. Though it may be hard for her to watch her husband getting immersed in an interest she cannot share, it can be even more upsetting—for both of them—to turn his source of pleasure into a test of their marital compatibility.

It would be far better for a wife in this position to find an activity of her own—something that gives her as much pleasure and sense of involvement as her husband's gives him. If she has children of school age, it could be something she does during the day. If her children are still small, it could be an evening or weekend activity. In this case, she might work out an arrangement with her husband whereby he agrees to look after the kids while she's out. A compromise of this kind, designed to ensure that she also gets a chance to become involved in something not connected with the home, can make it a lot easier for her to accept the time he devotes to his hobby.

My husband is insanely jealous. Though I've never given him any cause to doubt my love and fidelity, he suspects my every move. He won't take me to parties and he doesn't like me to go out with my girlfriends. I'm beginning to feel like a prisoner in my own home. How can I possibly get him to trust me?

A little jealousy on the part of one's mate can, of course, be flattering and gratifying. But when a loved one's jealousy becomes obsessive, it ceases to be reassuring, and becomes deeply distressing.

After two years of marriage, Kate was reaching the end of her tether. Her husband Gary was jealous of every single person she was fond of, from her parents and sisters, to her neighbors and girlfriends. It didn't even stop there. He was always convinced that she was hiding some secret romance from him, and he cross-questioned her endlessly about her daily activities. Every letter she received had to pass his inspection, and he always answered the phone when he was at home, in case it might be "the other man."

Despite this badgering, Kate adored her husband, and knew in her heart that he felt guilty about not trusting her. But his groundless jealousy was getting worse and worse. When she tried laughing away his fears, she only succeeded in offending him. When she tried logical arguments, he just retaliated with still more vehement accusations. At last, to please him, she tried limiting her contacts with others—refusing invitations, and adopting a rather cold and unfriendly attitude toward friends and neighbors. Even this didn't work. In fact, it seemed to make Gary more suspicious than ever. Why? Because he interpreted the change in her attitude as a final proof that she really did have something to hide.

In desperation, Kate went to a marriage guidance counselor, who surprised her by suggesting an entirely new way of tackling the problem. "So long as you are truly worthy of trust," said the counselor, "you would be unwise to alter your normal behavior in any way. Succumbing to Gary's jealousy will help neither you nor him. Even if he could lock you up in a tower, like the princess in the fairy tale, he would still worry. Why? Because his irrational jealousy probably has less to do with you than with some deep-seated insecurity he feels. Let's try to discover where it all began."

Together, Kate and the counselor explored the possible reasons for Gary's feelings. Kate knew that he had been brought up by his father because his mother had left the family when he was a little boy. Never before, however, had Kate seen any connection between this unhappy event and her present problem. But, as the counselor pointed out, his mother's desertion might be the key to Gary's anxiety about Kate. He might well be afraid that she, like his mother, would one day betray his trust. If so, his excessive jealousy was simply an expression of that basic fear.

Again, the counselor stressed that Kate should not alter her whole personality to please her husband. What she must do instead was to accept the reality of his feelings, and show him that she understood and took them seriously. At the same time, however, she should maintain her right to be the same warm, outgoing person he fell in love with. Only by combining understanding with personal honesty could she begin to help him conquer his problem.

This was sound advice, but, as Kate found, it took a great deal of patience and tact to carry out. Deep-seated anxieties like Gary's take a long time to overcome. But it *is* possible to overcome them. Where there is love, there can also be trust, even if it has to be learned, slowly but surely, over a period of time.

Marital
Teamwork

I'm married to a man who simply refuses to lift a finger around the house. All he does when he comes home is sink into a chair and watch TV, while I go on working—making dinner and washing the dishes, giving the kids their baths and putting them to bed, finishing the washing and ironing, etc. He won't help me because he sees all this as "woman's work." How on earth can I get him to lend a hand?

The first and most important hurdle to get over in a situation like this is the masculine assumption that all chores within the home are "feminine." But very few men can be persuaded to be more helpful by wifely nagging or lecturing. One wife who tried to change her husband's attitude by preaching the doctrines of Women's Lib to him, only succeeded in rousing his fury at the very idea of Women's Liberation. A better tactic is to appeal to two of his weak spots—his children's need for him as their father, and his pride in his own strength. When it comes to dealing with the kids in the evening, she can encourage him to play his part in looking after them by assuring him that they need his masculine influence. She might tell him that, by doing more with them and for them, he can strengthen their love and respect for him. It's a rare man who, deep down, doesn't care deeply about what his children think of him.

As for the other point—appealing to his male ego as physically strong—many women have found that they can get their husbands to help out with the kind of chores that require a lot of sheer bodily energy and power. Such things as floor polishing, window washing, taking the laundry to the laundramat, doing the weekly grocery shopping, —even doing the dishes if there are stacks and stacks of them—can be seen as "man's work" just because they require so much stamina. If a woman can organize her chores in such a way as to leave these heavier duties to her husband, she can help him see that his particular talents are absolutely essential in running the home they share.

Few women are blessed with a husband like the one who assured his wife, soon after the birth of their first child, that from then on he would share any task that had to be done after the normal nine-to-five working day. But, with a little tact and the right approach, most wives can get their husbands to participate more in the activities that make a man's home his castle.

My husband behaves like a different person toward me when we're out together. At home he treats me like an equal, listens to what I have to say, and often asks my advice about things. But when we're with other people, he seems to get a kick out of putting me down. I feel so humiliated when this happens. What makes him act this way?

Curiously enough, the reason may lie in the fact that a wife's presence can pose a kind of threat to a man's confidence in himself. At work, or out with the boys, he can think of himself as strong, independent, the master of his own destiny. At home alone with his wife, he can let down his defenses and be the person he really is (which, to some extent of course, is vulnerable and dependent.) When he and his wife are together in the presence of other people, however, he may find it difficult to reconcile these two images of himself. In this situation, he may feel the need to prove himself the stronger partner, and wind up hurting his wife's feelings in the process.

Bob was one such husband—easy-going at home, but domineering in company. "One night after a party," says his wife Sue, "I finally let him have it. He'd spent the entire evening regaling everybody with stories about what a dumb bunny I am. And every time I tried to put in *my* two cents' worth, he either interrupted me, contradicted me, or both. By the time we got home I was good and mad. I ranted and raved about how he always made a fool of me in public, and said I'd never go anywhere with him again if he didn't stop it. I guess I really took him by surprise. At first, he said he didn't know what I was talking about, but then I gave him some concrete examples from that very evening, and he had to agree that I was probably right. The upshot was that he promised to check that impulse to 'kid' me (as he likes to call it) in company. And you know, he really does try. It still happens sometimes, but when it does, I catch his eye and give him a wink. It's a kind of private signal between us. He usually winks back and changes the subject. Just knowing that he understands how I feel and is ready to respond has made our social life a lot more enjoyable for me."

Many husbands, like Bob, are honestly unaware of this tendency to belittle their wives in company. In such cases, it is better for a wife to air her grievance than to play the silent martyr. Mutual understanding about such things is essential if a couple are to operate as a team in social situations.

I don't get any help from my husband in disciplining the children. He's always saying I should take a firmer hand with them, but believe me, he's the one who spoils them. When he's home, he lets them break every rule in the book. How can I get him to stop playing the perpetual good guy, and help me lay down the law to the kids?

It's a rare husband and wife who agree absolutely about how and when to discipline their children. Probably the most commonly heard complaint is that one parent is too lenient with them, while the other is forced into the role of meanie. More often than not, it's the wife who gets stuck with this role, because she's the one who's in charge of the children most of the time. Of course, to a large extent, she cannot avoid being their lawmaker and policewoman—it is simply part of her role as mother. But she does have every right to ask for her husband's co-operation and support in dealing with them when he is at home. This is not to suggest that she ever use the "wait till your father comes home" approach. That tactic can only demonstrate her own inability to cope with the kids, and worse, encourage them to see their father in an unfavourable light. And it goes without saying that the last thing a man wants to do at the end of a long hard day is to punish his children for something they did hours ago while he was away. But if a man seems to be reluctant to assume any responsibility for disciplining the children when he is at home, he is opting out of something they not only need, but expect from him. In a case like this, a wife should make it clear to him that the children will love and respect him far more if he shows them that he is willing to be tough when it is necessary. A wife and her husband should always try to reach some agreement about how to handle certain disciplinary problems—and then stick to it. Children who see that their parents are prepared to present a united front when it comes to discipline tend to feel more secure, and are certainly less likely to try playing one parent off against the other. As child studies clearly demonstrate, children need not only love, but definite rules of behavior backed up by both parents.

With every passing year, my husband gets more difficult about money. I try my best to keep within our budget, but he's never satisfied, and criticizes me constantly about my spending. It's not that he isn't earning enough for our needs. So why this "charity stops at home" routine?

Marriage counselors cite money as one of the most common causes of marital friction. Possibly this is because in the majority of marriages, it is the husband who must earn the money, the wife who must spend it—on food, clothing, and all the other things the family needs. There are wives, of course, who do fall into the spendthrift category. But the majority are doing their level best to make ends meet—and, as we all know, it takes a good deal of skill these days to stretch the ever-shrinking dollar. But a man who is out working all week may not be fully aware of just how fast prices are really rising. Alarmed at the speed with which his hard-earned salary gets spent, he may become convinced that his wife is being careless, even extravagant, and start nagging at her to economize. This problem can be exaggerated if he is a man who tends to be overcautious by nature, or who has learned the hard lesson of "waste not, want not," as a child. With such a man, it can be difficult to arrive at a good working arrangement about family finances. But it can be done. Here's how one women did it.

"From the very outset of our marriage," says Joanne, a housewife of 29, "Jack had been very careful with money. But as long as I was working, it didn't seem to matter; with two salaries coming in, I guess he felt secure enough. We had to cut back, of course, when I stopped working and had the children. But by then Jack was doing a lot better at work, so I thought everything would be O.K. I was wrong. He started accusing me of mismanaging the money he gave me, and demanding lengthy explana-

tions of why this or that purchase was necessary. After a while, I began to feel so guilty about spending money that I didn't dare buy anything that wasn't strictly necessary. Then one day I caught sight of myself in the mirror. I looked downright shabby. 'This is ridiculous,' I said to myself. 'If I'm too scared of Jack and his budget to buy even a few things for myself, I'll just have to find a way to go back to work.'

"That night I had a long talk with him. Instead of being on the defensive about money the way I had been, I took a firm, positive approach. First, I insisted on knowing exactly how much he was earning—would you believe, I hadn't dared to ask before?—and then I told him that I simply must have some money to spend on myself without feeling guilty about it. I would take a part-time job if necessary, I said. In the meantime, I told him that it would help me a lot if he could do some of the bargain hunting, particularly when it came to things like replacing worn-out appliances and so forth.

"I think it really amazed him, my taking this direct, positive approach to our finances, but it worked. He wouldn't hear of my getting a job, especially as he knew I didn't really want to, and, of his own accord, he suggested quite a generous sum for me to spend as I saw fit. 'Joanne's money,' as we now call the regular amount I have to spend as I choose, has already done a lot to restore my sense of being an equal, trusted partner in our relationship. As for Jack, he really has proved a big help in finding the best *and* cheapest buys on the market. Meeting this kind of challenge is really his strong point, and he actually seems to enjoy it. Moreover, it makes him far more aware of the grim realities of soaring prices, and helps him to understand what I'm up against. In fact, I think we both feel more like equal partners in the money game these days. It's become a problem we share, rather than something we argue about. The difference that has made to our marriage is amazing. A year ago, I never would have believed we could talk about money as calmly as we do today."

Sexual Harmony

Our sex life is going downhill fast, and my husband says it's all my fault. I just see it as a chore, he says, and try to get out of it all the time. But after coping with the kids all day, I really don't feel much like a sex kitten at night. Besides, it makes me kind of mad sometimes to think that I'm expected to make love whenever he feels like it, just because I'm his wife. Still, if things go on like this, I'm afraid I'll lose him. What can I do?

This might well be the most widespread marital problem of all—and not surprisingly, for it is in the marriage bed that the delicate balance of give and take between husband and wife can be most easily lost. Without thinking much about it, a man may indeed get into the habit of expecting his wife to be ready for love whenever he is, while she may begin to resent her apparent lack of choice in the matter, and decide that he is being selfish. Afraid to say "no," but annoyed at being expected to say "yes" all the time, a wife may begin to make excuses, may even start exhausting herself with her daily chores on purpose, in order to have a valid excuse for being unresponsive at night. Saying "no" can be a woman's way of rebelling against being taken for granted; of testing, or punishing her husband; of asserting her individuality; even of expressing doubts about her own capacity for giving and receiving sexual pleasure. The only trouble is that by saying "no" to her husband, she is also saying "no" to herself, and denying her own needs.

Perhaps the first step for any woman facing this basic problems is to reexamine her own feelings about herself and her husband. If her reluctance stems from the fact that she has begun to see sex as just another wifely duty, she might remind herself that married love is meant to be a source of pleasure and fulfillment for her, as well as for her husband. One tried and true way of restoring the balance of physical love between them is for her to take the initiative from time to time—rather than merely saying "yes" or "no" to him. Many women have found that by initiating lovemaking themselves, they not only feel more like equal partners, but also find a renewed sense of enjoyment in bed.

If, as often happens, a woman finds that she cannot respond to her husband because she feels angry, another approach can be tried. Stifled hostilities have a notorious way of surfacing at precisely the moment when a woman knows she should feel loving and giving, and the very conflict between desire and annoyance can make sexual enjoyment impossible. If and when this happens, one thing she can do is suggest that she and her husband get up, go into the living room, and discuss the matter—and then go back to bed together. The first time this happens, he may be rather taken aback, but most husbands can see the value of having a wife who feels truly loving, even if it means that she has to get something off her chest first. The main thing is that all quarrels and grievances be settled outside, rather than inside, the bedroom.

If sexual difficulties have arisen because a wife feels she has lost the capacity to enjoy physical love, she may find that the road back lies, first and foremost, in rediscovering her own sensuality. How? By allowing herself to relish such simple pleasures as the luxury of a long, relaxing bath, the warmth of the sun or the feel of cool sheets on her skin, the smell of fresh bread, fruit, or flowers, the rhythm of music, and the exhilaration of sheer physical movement. These are all sensual pleasures she enjoyed without thinking twice about it in childhood. As an adult, she may find—and many other women have —that by putting herself back in touch with her senses, she also reawakens her desire for the more intense pleasures of her sexual relationship.

When a woman begins to regard her bedroom as a place where *two* can love and be loved, give and receive pleasure, she often discovers to her delight that she is rarely too tired for lovemaking with her husband.

I just don't understand my husband. Recently, he's started asking me to do an elaborate striptease for him before we make love. Who does he think I am —Belle Star? I feel silly doing that kind of thing, but when I refuse, he gets all upset, and says I don't really love him. What I'm beginning to wonder is, does he really love me?

This complaint comes from a woman who has been happily married for five years. But it's an issue that can arise at any stage in a marriage. Joan, 24, had only been married three months when her husband Tony shyly presented her with a pair of black stockings and a frilly garter belt, and asked her to put them on before they went to bed. Peggy, after ten years of marriage, couldn't believe her ears when her normally undemanding spouse suggested that they try making love in the family car. Susan, newly pregnant,

was embarrassed and insulted when her husband asked her to wear a see-through blouse without a bra during a quiet evening at home.

All these women were deeply distressed by what they considered an abnormal request on the part of their husbands. But when they showed a reluctance to comply, their husbands were obviously hurt and angry.

The conflict involved here goes back to a fundamental difference in the way men and women regard sex. For a woman, making love is just that: a physical expression of mutual desire and affection. She usually has fairly fixed ideas about what is right and proper in sex—ideas which do not include "unnecessary" erotic embellishments. Asked to incorporate such extras into her lovelife, she may feel degraded, as though her own unadorned presence, in her own comfortable bedroom, was insufficient to arouse her husband's desire. What she, like many women, may fail to realize is that men often yearn for a hint of wickedness in the women they love. Certainly, as decent, respectable men, they want their wives to be decent, respectable women—at least in public. But in private, they sometimes want an added spice of eroticism to heighten their enjoyment of sex. In fact, what men often want their wives to be is the perfect combination of "naughty but nice."

Many a woman will indulge her husband's whims simply to please him, and this is fine for a start. But if she is truly to enjoy the proceedings herself, she must appreciate that it is *her* body, artfully concealed, slowly revealed, or seen in unaccustomed surroundings, that excites him. As most women would agree, the power to go on being exciting to their husbands can be a very real source of pleasure to themselves. A few perceptive women have even discovered an added source of pleasure in persuading their husbands to return the favor in kind. One woman, for example, agreed to perform the striptease her husband wanted if he would do the same for her. The benefits of this ingenious suggestion were twofold. His initial embarrassment gave him a valuable insight into the way his wife had felt at first about doing it for him. On her side, this special demonstration of his love for her proved unexpectedly exciting.

Thus, though a husband and wife may sometimes approach their sex life with seemingly opposed expectations, they can, with a little mutual give and take, find a solution that is satisfying to them both.

Some time ago I began to suspect that my husband was being unfaithful to me when he went away on his sales trips. One day I finally came right out and accused him of it. You should have seen his face—he looked like the little boy who's been caught with his hand in the cookie jar. He admitted to being unfaithful a couple of times, but he said all the guys did it. The girls were just pick-ups who didn't mean anthing to them. He kept repeating that he loved me, and that nothing had changed between us. I don't agree. How can I go on living with a man I can't trust?

Marital confrontations of this kind take place in millions of homes every year. Men have an unfortunate tendency to yield to temptation, and their wives have an uncanny knack of finding out about it. Though no one really knows the extent of male infidelity, the Kinsey report was probably not far wrong in estimating that about 50 per cent of all husbands are unfaithful at some point in their married lives. Why do they do it? The reasons are as varied as the men themselves.

For some, like the husband described above, infidelity is a sort of occupational hazard. Away from his wife for a period of days or even weeks, and under pressure from his pals to live it up a little, a husband may indeed do just that, in the sincere belief that such isolated incidents cannot harm his marriage. Other men play a riskier game when they engage in actual affairs—however brief—closer to home. In doing so, they

may unconsciously be trying to prove that they are still as exciting and desirable as they were before they married, or even striving to enhance their status in the eyes of other men. By plunging into this kind of illicit adventure, they may also be seeking a means of escape from the inevitable monotony of everyday life. In some cases, they may even be looking for a way to get back at their wives for some unresolved conflict or disappointment in their marriage.

It has often been said that a husband's unfaithfulness is the result, rather than the cause, of marital disharmony. On this assumption, the advice usually given to the wife is that she must re-examine their marriage and put right what has gone wrong. But many experts disagree with this approach. Infidelity, they point out, has been known to occur in even the happiest of marriages. Thus, although complete fidelity would seem to be the cornerstone of the mutual trust so vital to a lasting relationship, it must be said that both good and bad marriages can be hit by this kind of betrayal.

Of course the discovery of a husband's unfaithfulness must force a wife to reappraise her relationship with him. But if she values her man and her marriage—as well as her own self-esteem—she must also bear in mind that an infidelity on his part need not mean a rejection of either herself or their marriage. In fact, the well-known male capacity for separating love and sex, and for prizing home and family above all else, can be her best ally and protector against this kind of threat to her security. This is not to say, of course, that any woman should force herself to tolerate a husband's unfaithfulness. He must be made aware that, by betraying her trust, he is putting their entire relationship at risk. If, through discussion and genuine heart-searching, he can realize this, understand her point of view, and come to terms with the reasons behind his infidelity, there is a real possibility that this challenge to their happiness can be the beginning of a new commitment to each other and their life together.

Conflicts Over Work

My husband seems to be reaching a dead end in his job. No matter how hard he works, he doesn't get promoted, and he's beginning to see himself as a failure. I give him all the encouragement I can, but he never follows my advice. It's getting so he won't even talk about it any more. Doesn't he want me to take an interest in his career?

The answer to this woman's question might be both "yes" and "no." It depends on what kind of interest she's taking. There are many men who simply don't thrive on constant encouragement and suggestions about how to get ahead at work. Quite understandably, they interpret this kind of interest as out-and-out nagging. In the case above, it sounds as though that might be exactly what this wife has been doing, however unknowingly. The old saying about how there's a woman behind every successful man can be taken too far, and without realizing it, a wife can make her husband feel that he's not living up to her expectations. This kind of added pressure can make it difficult for him to succeed under even the best circumstances. Perhaps the best thing she can do is to let him know that she thinks the world of him, and that, whatever he choses to do, or not to do, about his job is all right with her. This can make an impressive difference in the way her husband feels about himself and his progress at work.

Anne found this out after a few years of trying in vain to be helpful to her husband Derek. She had thought that a good wife ought to be in there pitching, always ready to give her support, concern, and advice. But somehow, her wifely interest didn't seem to be helping him at all. In fact, it got to the point where she could almost see him wince when the subject of his job came up. He worked long hours, but he wasn't getting anywhere. Was he hiding something from her? She knew he confided in his brother Alec, so one day she called him and asked him what was happening. Was Derek worried about getting fired? Was his boss taking him for granted? Was he in the right job after all? Alec didn't pull any punches. "Anne," he said, "I think the trouble is that you've been nagging at him too much. He's working as hard as he can, but he says you're never satisfied. You're determined to make him a success, and he doesn't think he has it in him. Why don't you try just letting up on him for a while?"

Anne was flabberghasted. All she'd done, she protested, was show a little interest in what her husband was doing. But she decided to follow Alec's advice. She not only stopped asking Derek about how things were going at work all the time, but also found an opportunity to tell him how glad she was that he was married to her, and *not* to his job. She even suggested that he stop putting in all that overtime work and start spending more time with her and the girls. The effect this had on her husband surprised even Alec. Derek began to relax and be more like his

141

old confident, easy-going self. Somehow, this change in his attitude came across at work as well, and it wasn't long before he was offered a new position with his company that upped his status considerably. Anne was delighted, and told him so. But she refrained from offering any advice or suggestions. As she herself puts it: "When he can manage so well for himself, he doesn't need anything more from me than my respect and pride in him."

My children are at school now, and I want very much to go back to work. But my husband keeps raising objections about how the children still need me, and how tired I'll be, and how we don't need the extra money I'd earn anyway. But with the youngsters away all day, I feel I'm just turning into a cabbage. I've just got to get out of the house and into the world again. How can I get him to see my point of view?

Despite the growing number of working wives and mothers, some women still find it difficult to convince their husbands that going out to work is not going to mean the end of a happy home life. A husband who resists his wife's desire to get out of the house and into a job may have various reasons for wanting to keep her at home. He may feel that it would damage his image as head of the household to have a working wife. Some men do equate their masculine role with being the sole breadwinner. He may also feel that, once outside the tidy world of home and family, she will be led astray by some office Don Juan and be unfaithful to him. For some men, the very idea of a woman being out at work all day—expecially if she is a warm, outgoing person by nature—spells danger. It can also be very difficult for a man to see his wife as an independent person with special needs and talents that don't find full expression in the home. Isn't she satisfied? he may ask himself. What does she want? A woman with a husband reluctant for her to go out to work must realize that this new desire of hers can pose quite an unexpected threat to his whole view of himself, their marriage, and her.

He may not readily acknowledge this, however, and instead throw up a barrage of seemingly practical reasons why she should stay at home. How will she manage if one of the kids get sick and needs her? Does she realize how difficult it will be to get through the housework plus a day at the office or factory? Besides, he's already earning enough to support the family, and she'll probably not make enough after taxes to make all the upheaval in their lives worthwhile.

Faced with such objections, a woman may feel overwhelmed with guilt, and wonder if she's just being selfish about wanting a job, be it part time or full time. In such a situation, she must realize that many other women have done this before her, and that she, like them, has a right, as well as a need, to fulfill herself as an individual. If she feels confident that she can handle both a job and her role as wife and mother, she will simply have to persist in her ambition, and hope that, by discussion and reassurance, she can ultimately get her husband to agree. It may require patience, and it may require proof. She can, for example, suggest to her husband that she merely give it a try and see how it works out. If it proves too hard, or too upsetting for the family as a whole, she will be willing to give it up until such time as it is easier for all concerned. But she must make it clear to him that working does not necessarily have to detract from her role as wife and mother. There are many jobs these days flexible enough to allow a woman time off for school vacations, for example. Moreover, it can be pointed out that having a job can give her added incentive to organize her household chores more efficiently. It may also help to make it clear that her earnings will be used strictly for extras—luxuries, not necessities. This can reassure a man that his wife is in no doubt about his ability to provide for the family's basic needs. Finally, one of the most important things to get over to a husband dubious about his wife's working is that she needs to feel that she, too, has something to contribute to their life together—not merely as a homemaker, but also as a happy and interesting companion to him.

With each new promotion he gets, I feel more inadequate. I know he expects me to keep up with him by being up-to-date, well-dressed, good at entertaining important people, and all that, but I don't think I can do it. That's just not me. Why can't he just let me go on being a wife and mother?

Some wives leap at the chance to prove how well they can keep up with their husbands' changing job status. Others, like the wife above, feel frightened and resentful about it. Indeed, it can be quite upsetting for a woman who has spent years at home caring for her children to find herself suddenly being thrust into the new and demanding role of "business asset" to her husband. It can be all the harder if, over the years, she has let herself get more or less out of touch with the world beyond her own community.

In many ways, of course, her problem is similar to that of the wife who wants to—or has to—go back to work after years of being a full time housewife. For both, it's a question of getting back into the world outside where the pace is faster and the level of sophistication higher. In both cases, a woman can feel worried that she hasn't the self-confidence, the skills, or the social know-how to compete, and shrink at the very prospect of putting herself to the test. It's a very understandable feeling, but one she should really try to overcome—if for no other reason than to enlarge her own scope and self-image. After all, the day is bound to come when her children grow up and no longer need her full time attention. When that day arrives, she may well find herself wishing that she had not dropped out of the race so completely when she was younger. Thus, the challenge of keeping up with a husband's changing status at work can be a valuable opportunity to prepare for the time when a woman wants to have new interests and new ways of fulfilling herself anyway.

Being ready to change and adapt can make the transition from housewife to business helpmeet much easier. Ellen, the mother of three teenage children, discovered this when her husband Peter, after years of hard work as a salesman for a major appliance firm, was made area manager. Practically overnight, they both found themselves hurtled into an entirely different social scene from the one they were used to. They moved into a new house in a new town, and began entertaining various executives and their wives. It was easier for Peter, of course, because his job put him on an equal footing with these people, and he had business to discuss with them. But Ellen felt scared and inadequate about playing this new role. Did the house look nice enough? Was her cooking up to scratch? Did the new clothes she had bought really suit her? Anxiously, she asked Peter for reassurance, and got it, on all counts but one. "Honey," he said, "you're doing absolutely great, and I couldn't feel more proud of you. But why don't you talk more? You don't have to sit there as quiet as a mouse. You have just as much to say as any of these people." Ellen, however, was convinced she had nothing to contribute to the conversation. She certainly couldn't talk about child-raising all the time. So she decided to put something new into her life that she *could* talk about. She had loved acting at school years ago, so she joined the local drama club, and got Peter to take her to the theatre more often. In addition, she began participating in the local community action group. Both interests offered her new scope for talents she had almost forgotten she had, and she soon began to feel not only more self-confident, but positively younger than she had in years. No longer did she worry about having something to contribute to a conversation with Peter's business associates. In fact, she found herself wondering from time to time why *their* wives were so dull. As Peter put it one evening after a company get-together, "Ellen, you thought you were going to find it hard to keep up with me. I'm beginning to worry that I won't be able to keep up with you!"

For Your Bookshelf

Males and Females
by Corinne Hutt, Penguin Books, Inc. (Baltimore, Maryland: 1972); Penguin Books, Ltd. (London; 1972)

Men in Groups
by Lionel Tiger, Random House, Inc. (New York: 1969); Thomas Nelson and Sons, Ltd. (London: 1970)

The Male Attitude
by Charles W. Ferguson, Little, Brown and Company (Boston, Massachusetts: 1966)

The Changing Roles of Men and Women
by Edmund Dahlstrom, Beacon Press (Boston, Massachusetts: 1971); Gerald Duckworth and Company, Ltd. (London: 1970)

Men and Marriage
by Heather Jenner and Muriel Segal, G. P. Putnam's Sons (New York: 1970); Michael Joseph, Ltd. (London: 1970)

Marriage and Family Relationships
by Richard H. Klemer, Harper and Row Publishers, Inc. (New York: 1970)

Male and Female
by Margaret Mead, William Morrow and Company, Inc. (New York: 1949); Penguin Books, Ltd. (London: 1962)

The Manipulated Man
by Esther Vilar, translated by Eva Borneman, Abelard-Schuman, Ltd. (New York: 1972); Abelard-Schuman, Ltd. (London: 1972)

Picture Credits